MASKED
DEPRAVITY

MASKED DEPRAVITY:

Poverty Row Mexican Wrestling/ Horror Films from New Jersey and their Role in the Pollution of Children's Minds. A cinematic handbook of incompetence

Andre Perkowski

To order additional copies of this book, contact:
Xlibris Corporation
1-888-7-XLIBRIS
www.Xlibris.com
Orders@Xlibris.com

INTRODUCTION.

The El Intoxico Saga: features torn directly from an abused part of the brain. Impaired mexican wrestling mayhem in a no holds barred atmosphere of "what the hell?". Noise music tinted and reshuffled for maximum ear-market penetration–EL INTOXICO: the ultimate superhero of nonexistent ideals.

Catch the excitement.

Smell the entertainment.

This book includes the original scripts that were forgotten and improvised away as the two extant Intoxico epics, "Contra El Cerebro De Hitler" and "Contra El Vicio Infernale".

Appendixes are provided in the form of press release and propaganda material developed by strict perverts of no fixed ability.

In addition, raw brainstorming session notes with G. Groy, The Spirit of Santo, Dr. Anne Gora at the Wood Institute of Glandular Research, and other noted trash culture notables. Please squint and skip past these sessions.

In addition, the raw production diary journal kept by production manager Lucien Oullette are extracted from and pared down for "Satan's Brevity".

We thank you for your wise investment.

Please consult bowleggedmanmedia.com for further instructions. Some of you may notice that the released films in no way resemble these scripts. You may have noticed that this first edition is missing several advertised items. Yes–"must be is".

Sincerely,

Coleman T. Craig

BMMedia Consumption Liason

http://bowleggedmanmedia.com

CHAPTER ONE.

Prelude–Ballyhoo–Pitch–Info–Enjoy!

Yes, EL INTOXICO. That loveable masked Mexican hero that teaches us all a little bit about life in modern times. Two-fisted trash handcrafted by only the finest old world craftsmen. Low in fat, high in violence. They don't make them like this anymore for a DAMN GOOD REASON. Find out why and why not by clicking ferociously. EL INTOXICO: the first film. Cursed from day one, yet completed in spite of the trauma. EL INTOXICO Y BLUE BASTARD CONTRA EL CEREBRO DE HITLER: the sequel that does everything the first film didn't care to. Like being shot on actual film. RIDICULOUS COLORS! Mad science. MAYHEM IN THE NAME OF PROGRESS! More excrement than any major Hollywood studio dares to present. Available in mild or hot.
DANGEROUS! OBSCENE! UNRATED! UNCENSORED!

CHAPTER TWO.

"El Intoxico Contra El Cerebro de Hitler" (2000)

A TENDER story about a mad doctor, half genius, half lunatic; and his experiments in living flesh: perversions beyond comprehension!

A fiendish plot to revive the brain of a dictator and create an army of ferocious apes!

COLOR! UNCUT! ALL TRUE!

Murder! Immolation! Lobotomy! Pipe Organs! A bloodmaddened despot of perversion, Doctor Irving Franquestein! BRUTAL WRESTLING! ILLEGAL MUTILATIONS!

El Intoxico rends the screen limb from limb with SHEER CHARISMA!

Sequel? Prequel?

What relation does this film have to the original EL INTOXICO?

WE DON'T KNOW! YOU DON'T KNOW!

But you WANT TO KNOW—and you will—SOON! THIS YEAR!

COMING FALL 2000

from BOWLEGGED MAN MEDIA

Santo was but a light snack compared to the bloated HORROR of . . . EL INTOXICO.

EL CEREBRO DE HITLER CAST LIST

el intoxico as himself

blue bastard as himself

katie dugan as shirley gomez

adam leavitt as dr. irving franquestein
mr. unknown as himself
demonia del fuego as herself
evil dick, jr. as an ape
many other citizens as apes
sandy something as the virgin mary
david hayes as doctor gomez
chris roy as lt. terry brooks
jeff orig as mr. hopping vampire
hayden davis as the bisexual lab assistant
ofelia castillo as mrs. intoxico
adolf hitler as himself
caifano perkowitz as general smith
conrad brooks as a sweaty drunk with bad hair
drew tungsten as el hombre mono
ron campos as el hombre standin
joe linett as un hipster
daniel j. smith as otro hipster
los rompecabazas de satanas as themselves
crew
sound design by rodney voisine
music by the farmingdale sound machine, the inhibitors, spin
cycle
and public domain
edited by ontor pertawst
assistant director dick trent
mexican wrestling consultant el boracho
liquor liason richard lepis
reel to reel consultant virgilio castillo
production manager lucien oullette
director of photography russ tambien
gaffer ernesto pobrecito
executive kali ramon
key grip leon machin
written, produced, and directed by

andre perkowski
El Intoxico, famous masked Mexican wrestler and philosophical psychopath of the apocalypse. You knew that.
See him now in blazing color! Weird! Beyond tragic! Destructive! Original! Potent! The ultimate atrocity . . .
90 minutes long . . . yet it seems to last for 3 days.
EL CEREBRO DE HITLER
A pertinent motion picture about modern problems, featuring BRAND NEW musical contributions from troubled children.
Explosions! HOPPING VAMPIRES! SKULLS! A fiendish scientist that licks ventriloquist dummies! HORRIBLE! Despicable!
DTs . . . overindulgence . . . liver transplants . . . a poignant vision of a world torn apart by the misuse of technology . . . repulsive yet inevitable . . . a triumph of the human spirit!
More AROUSING than the leading brand. SOOTHING—CALMING . . . erects and prolongs for your pleasure.
Golly gee, virginal Kodak 16mm Vision stock with blindingly hallucinatory colors! Rinse hands and powder eyes before viewing! Luxury—convenience . . . WEIRD SEX IN A MAELSTORM OF DESPAIR! The movie that dares to imply that there are breasts in this world. UNFLINCHING! Yet all too REAL! This is it: the film that shows it all.
EL INTOXICO
y Blue Bastard
CONTRA
EL CEREBRO DE HITLER
a film of mexican masked intrigue
by
andre perkowski
FADE IN
EXT. STOCK FOOTAGE
Clips of various "horror" themed snippets from old movies and outtakes cut back and forth. Generic "creepy" organ music simpers on the soundtrack as an urgent narrator starts babbling nonstop.

NARRATOR

This film is devoted to that hour of the morning when reality and nightmare merge into one . . . when the monsters and illusions of darkness remain lodged within the horrified skull . . . when the howl of the wolf chills the body into spasms of terror and ultimate dread . . . . It is the hour of the nightmare . . . Once this land of monstrous nightmare is entered, no one can say when a return to the normal will occur. Suffice to say that those who watch this film with this knowledge fully implanted within their minds. For this film is not a record of mere death and unheard of sexual atrocity . . . but a vision into that twilight of sanity where nothing exists within the frame of human reason. All that shall be heard and seen here will take you into the desert of the soul, where mortals dare not venture . . . It is through this film that the ultimate in horror will be yours to know . . . and hopefully you will return to tell of your lust ridden voyage. As you journey into this maze of howling terror remember that the forces at work are to be respected . . .

Lightning crash.

NARRATOR

For the power of darkness is the mightiest on earth. And those who might scoff or sneer at their works become the next in line for the eternal nightmare . . . to dwell forever in the darkness where escape becomes only a struggle for survival against the monsters whose domain lies within this film.

Another lightning crash. Wipe to:

Start on the next line which is the first Slug line.

EXT. STOCK FOOTAGE

A barrage of recycled El Intoxico footage and animated titles fling themselves across the screen.

NARRATOR

Yes, El Intoxico! Idol of the multitudes and undisputed king of the art of Mexican drunken wrestling! Determination . . . Courage . . . and an impeccable sense of justice are all components of this fine citizen. Capable of impossible feats of drinking and the ultimate force for goodness and rightful doings! His friend . . . the trustworthy and always dependable BLUE BASTARD: el senor de azul . . . together for the first time in the most thrilling motion picture of all time . . . EL INTOXICO Y BLUE BASTARD CONTRA EL CEREBERO DE HITLER!

The title smashes into the screen. Fade out.

INT. MODEL—NIGHT

Fade in to a toy castle with dry ice smoke around it. More "sinister" organ chords rumble.

DISSOLVE TO:

INT. MARTUCCI'S LAB

Doctor Martucci performs a bit of mad science on a cheap set. A man in a very cheap monster mask lies on a table. Organ music continues droning. Doctor Martucci adjusts meaningless knobs and pours food coloring-laden chemicals from flask to flask. The lab set is clearly a kitchen with fake stone walls badly painted on white paper, skulls, broken computer equipment, wires, and many appliances.

NARRATOR

A diabolical tale of lust and horror . . . a harrowing narrative of passion and depravity. A sex-maddened professor-half-genius—half-lunatic-performs sickening experiments in living flesh . . . desperately seeking to slake his endless desire . . . only to find his results outdo his maddest dream!

Doctor Martucci laughs and faces the camera while standing over the monster on the table. His arms slowly rise as his ranting begins. He is also; like every other character in this film, poorly dubbed.

DOCTOR MARTUCCI

Tonight the blood of the innocents will flow and give rise to the ultimate in horror! You slumbered for centuries in the void of the ungood . . . now I summon you! The prophecies of the dark dominion known as dimension zero! The time is upon us . . . . awaken now, the monsters that reside in the dark! I call you to physical manifestation! That is my wish I tell you! Move about in the dark! Shudder to beingness! You will be nourished with human blood, imponderable king of witches and devilry!

The doctor stabs the victim with a knife that appears out of nowhere thanks to poor editing. Martucci cackles insanely as more stock footage lightning and thunder appear. Martucci continues laughing. For a very long time. Zoom in to his mouth and fade out.

INT. ARENA PHOTO

Fade in to a photo collage of of a mexican wrestling arena. "EL INTOXICO VS. YODOBO—LUCHA! BORACHO! EL SUPREMO!" proclaims the marquee. DISSOLVE TO:

INT. DRESSING ROOM

El Intoxico and Blue Bastard are sitting down in a dingy room with posters for Santo movies, El Intoxico I, and Espectros del Espacio on the wall. El Intoxico is dressed in his "wrestling" garb. What that consists of, I have no idea. Blue Bastard is in a sensible suit and turtleneck. His voice is a computer generated monotone to match his one-note personality. El Intoxico laughs and then speaks in a gruff bassy voice with odd pauses in mid sentence.

EL INTOXICO

Congra-duration, Blue Bastard. I know that you, like me, have decided to dedicate your life and your potent energies to serve the right of truth and power of good. Many dangers and many troubles await you in your task. Don't lose hope . . .

BLUE BASTARD

Thank you, El Intoxico. If I should need your help some time, tell me—can I count on you?

EL INTOXICO

I'll always be there by your side if you need me, my friend. But right now, I have to luchar in the ring.

BLUE DEMON

My friend . . . I tell you, good luck. But please . . . can you first tell me about how you adopted the mask and the fight for justice?

EL INTOXICO

I suppose I have time to go into . . . these details . . .

Music cue and atrocious gooey wipe to:

EXT. FIELD
El Intoxico wanders around. His face is not seen, and his body type is completely different from the guy in the previous scene.
EL INTOXICO (V.O.)
Yes . . . I was but a young man, interested in the criminal mind, but not prepared to take up an interest in justice. One day I began to experience strange stinging sensations in my brain . . .
El Intoxico continues walking around, his face is unseen . . . he starts clutching his brain and falling to the ground.
EL INTOXICO (V.O.)
I felt as if I were summoned to a special place, a holy place . . . indeed, the place most saturated in holiness in all of Mexico.
EXT. WEIRD ARCHY PARK BUILDING
El Intoxicotobe approaches a stone structure filled with arches. Out of nowhere a wizened Jesus in ridiculous clothing appears. Trumpet blast as he strikes some sort of odd expression or raises an eyebrow.
Jesu Christo then begins to teleport through the magic of stopmotion semianimation from doorway to doorway accompanied by a puff of smoke and a dumb sound effect. Finally he appears a few feet from El Intoxico.
JESU CHRISTO
My son, you have been preparing to take the road of vigilant observation. Not consciously, but in spirit. I've taught you to love the poor and the crippled and the weak and the degenerate, and now you are ready to help them and defend them, to fight for justice and the law of alcoholisms. And above all, to be the friend of the people and a true amigo del pueblo.
Angelic music rises as Jesus stretches out his hands. The Intoxico mask materializes into them. As he continues to speak, outtakes and footage from the first movie are shown briefly.
JESU CHRISTO
I am going to present you with this mask, which will be your pride and your emblem. When you put it on, you will have to honor it always and feel good about it, even when your own exist-

ence is endangered. If you feel capable of consecrating your life, swear to it now. But first, you have to know one thing: once you put it on, you can never go back to the world of the unmasked . . . Now tell me, are you willing?

EL INTOXICO

Yes right. This seems like a good thing for me to do at this point.

JESU CHRISTO

My son . . . do you know that you must never now do evil unto anyone, never deceive your men and fellows . . . dedicate your body and soul and liver as well to defending the weak and poverty stricken . . . implacably punish evil wherever you may find it. If you can't handle this task, burn the mask rather than let it fall into the ownership of the truly villanous!

EL INTOXICO

Yes . . . this I do gladly . . . for both Mexico and mankind!

JESU CHRISTO

El Intoxico, you must drink continuously and ferverently for 10 years I tell you-and the mask must always be upon you-even if you find a spouse, you must wait until your duty to the community is done before you take time for yourself and a family. Know this, El intoxico. Go now and fight those bad men who would give emotions and mankind a poor and ineloquent name!

EL INTOXICO

Yes . . . I swear it by my name, and my name is now El Intoxico! Thank you for showing me my task . . . and my future!

DISSOLVE TO:

INT. DRESSING ROOM

BLUE BASTARD

That's a fascinating story.

EL INTOXICO

My friend, not one goddamned word of it is a lie.

BLUE BASTARD

Right! That's why it is so fascinating!

EL INTOXICO

Yes . . . HAW HAW. I suppose you are right. My friend, it is time for me to luchar.

Intoxico gestures. WIPE TO:

INT. ARENA

El Intoxico enters the ring. His opponent, Commandante Murder (possibly in clown makeup or something equally dumb), is already in the ring, prancing and waving his arms around.

COMMANDANTE MURDER

You're nothing but pickles . . . you shitpiece, I'll rape you with my fists and show you that wrestling is never to be taken lightly!

El Intoxico just goes into a fighting stance and circles Commandante. The announcer is seated at a table with a very large and very fake microphone with TV call letters drawn on it in crayon. He sweats a lot and has the usual pencil thin moustache.

ANNOUNCER

El Intoxico, reigning champion of Mexican-style drunkard wrestling in a very deadly trap of carnage! But he has muscle mass and skeletal girth enough to withstand the pummeling blows of his opponent, Commandante Murder. The question is . . . who will be murdered? And how savage will it be? I love death!

The announcer continues in a random, stream of drunkenness way, describing the dull action as 2 men who obviously can't wrestle in the "traditional" way stumble around fake punching each other. Commandante Murder has a special move that consists of running into the ropes and falling down. Somehow Intoxico gets knocked out of the ring and against the announcer's table. He grabs the announcer's liquor and downs it in one gulp. Energized, he leaps into the ring and tears off Commandante's head or something. Abrupt cut to:

INT. DRESSING ROOM

Blue Bastard is reading a newspaper with a headline that screams KILLINGS AND BADNESS RAMPANT! El Intoxico enters and grabs a towel. He rubs it vigorously against his sweaty mask. Blue Bastard puts down the newspaper and smiles at Intoxico.

EL INTOXICO

Ah, but I love to defeat my enemies! HA HA HA HA!

BLUE BASTARD

You were unspeakably brutal, my friend!

EL INTOXICO

That's quite a compliment coming from you, Blue Bastard.

BLUE BASTARD

It's true what I say. By the way, my friend . . . have you heard about the killings? Yes. There is supernatural murder about . . .

EL INTOXICO

El Hombre . . . LOBO! AHGHGH! Yes, Shirley told me about it earlier before the bout.

BLUE BASTARD

That Shirley is a good woman . . . I would like to possess her.

EL INTOXICO

AHAHAHHA, my friend. Try, and I'll castrate you with your own fingers.

BLUE BASTARD

Yes! Let us have a good laugh!

Blue Bastard claps Intoxico on the back as he laughs a hollow robotic chuckle. Wipe to:

INT. BUDAN SET

"Budan" footage clumsily inserted with a new soundtrack.

NARRATOR

Bloodcrazed monsters seeking SAUSAGE carved from flesh! BUDAN! BUDAN! They cry BUDAN! Failed experiments . . . mishappen creatures . . .

EXT. OUTDOORS—NIGHT

Insert ancient Wuhrwolf footage featuring a drunken wolf halfheartedly attacking a few random dorks here.

NARRATOR

A ghoulish spectre of profanity, driven by lust and an insatiable appetite for . . . DEATH! Feasting on his prey . . . the foul HOMBRE LOBO!

INT. DOLE SET

Ancient Bob Dole/Murder footage.

NARRATOR

Malignant murders taking the form of trusted opionmakers and media pundits! Familiar death with an unpredictable outcome! Disgusting, bloody molestations! Terror beyond comprehension! Confusion without limits! Morals without a moment's restraint! A world of pungent pain and morbid mongrelization of all ethics . . .

EXT. STOCK FOOTAGE

WW II stock footage of explosions, Hitler, crowds, etc. followed by photos of Martucci/Franquestain.

NARRATOR

An insane war criminal wanted for the most depraved and unholy atrocities against his fellow man . . . a cursed scientist . . . a flawed theologist . . . Doctor Phillip Martucci . . . AKA Werner Krup . . . AKA . . . IRVING FRANQUESTAIN! Friend of Hitler. . . ENEMY of mankind! Wanted for MURDER . . . MANSLAUGHTER . . . RAPE . . . creation of unlicensed homunculi . . . NARCOTICS . . . and other sordid perversions . . . IRVING FRANQUESTAIN: Responsible for the outbreak of . . . MONSTROS!

The same damn footage of a lightning bolt cuts in.

INT. LAB

El Hombre Lobo is chained to a table. Martucci rants.

DOCTOR MARTUCCI

Silence! Calm yourself, Hombre Lobo! Do this as I will it! SILENCE! SILENCE! I will unleash you soon . . . soon, my precious monstruo . . . MUAHAHAH!

Int. CRENSHAW'S OFFICE/LAB—NIGHT

Crenshaw struts around a very poor looking lab set. He takes a few notes and peers into a microscope, then frowns and picks up a phone.

DOCTOR

Ah. Yes, hello. This is Doctor Abercrombie Crenshaw . . . I'm calling to see if you have any more declassified information available on the . . . German problem. Yes . . . Yes . . . Have they struck again?

INT. MILITAIRY BASE

A blank set with General Smith standing in the middle of it. He's talking on an antique phone while flipping through "Death of a Transvestite" in a bored manner.

GENERAL SMITH

HAW HAW HAW. Ah, you're STILL trying to scare everyone with your foolish little stories about Nazis? Sorry to mock your conclusions, Doctor . . . but please . . . this is the 20th century after all. Dead people don't leave their graves!

INT. LAB

DOCTOR

Don't count on it, General. I'm not talking about any sort of standard sexual deviant or graaave robber out there . . . These entities are obviously aliens! And the armed forces should indeed be looking out for them! These things are real, I've seen them . . . I've shown you the evidence that has a high degree of probable believability! Is it too difficult to believe? Three have already lost their lives . . . General . . . what will it take to convince you . . .

INT. MILITARY BASE

GENERAL

Doc, we've thoroughly investigated these preposterous claims of yours . . . . There are no Nazis, atomic or otherwise . . . No GERMAN MENACE . . . No Alien Reich is out there causing trouble. Those three murders are unrelated . . . And your so-called pictures and telometer readings are obviously falsified!

INT. LAB

DOCTOR

What? You dare accuse my scientific method of fraud? Why you slimy little man! Have it your way . . . . But when these Nazis continue to strike . . . you might just change your mind! Silly! GOOD DAY, SIR!

INT. MILITARY BASE

GENERAL

Heh. Thanks for the advice, doc. I've got a feeling we won't exactly be needing it. The united states military is competent enough in this matter and does not need the consultations you offer. You better watch out for little green men, Doctor!

The General cackles and hangs up the phone. LT. BROOKS approaches.

LT. BROOKS

Gee sir, but there is evidence of a German influence in these cases . . . don't you think Nazis might actually be involved?

GENERAL

Don't be so supersticious, Lt. Do you actually believe in Dimension Zero? Do you believe in little green men, too? There's just a disturbed citizen, probably some loathsome MINORITY, running around out there . . . that's the logical explanation.

LT. BROOKS

But why the hushup, sir? Why the media blanket?

GENERAL

National security, we're in charge . . . I'm in charge . . . uh, of this investigation and that's the way we operate. Now, get the hell out of my office and don't come back unless you have some REAL NEWS.

LT. BROOKS

Yessir. I still . . .

GENERAL

It's a joke . . . a gag . . . a prank! GET THE HELL OUT OF HERE!

INT. LAB

The Doctor slams a fist down on his desk.

DOCTOR

DAMN!

FADE OUT

INT. INTOXICO'S BEDROOM

FADE IN to a very cheap looking bedroom. Intoxico lies in bed. In his mask, of course. On his nightstand is a framed picture of El Santo. Over his bed is a massive crucifix. He yawns and gets

up slowly. Very bad music starts up as we begin the famous WAK-
ING UP MONTAGE as we see El Intoxico take a shower, sit on
the toilet while reading pornography, shave, get dressed in a snazzy
suit, etc.

INT. INTOXICO'S KITCHEN

Intoxico wanders down into a kitchen and fixes himself some
breakfast consisting of Frankenberry with Jack Daniels. After a few
spoonfulls, he gets up and heads toward the fridge. Upon opening
the fridge, a ridiculous monster pops out. They brawl and knock
over stuff until El Intoxico opens a drawer and takes out a huge
cardboard crucifix. The monster withers and finally Intoxico stabs
it in the chest and licks up the blood. DISSOLVE TO:

EXT. WOODS—NIGHT

A bad outdoor set with plastic trees and dry ice. Evil music
starts playing. Random Pedestrian John R. Citizen is strolling along
looking nervous. In the shadows and trees sinister, dark-cloaked
creatures can be seen. The shine of silver and glossy metal. CU of
an SS insignia and a Swastika armband. Whirring gears and clicks
indicating a robot or machine of some type. The Atomic Nazis
emerge, looking totally ridiculous, shiny and cardboardy. They
chase the citizen down the street and eviscerate him. Screams. The
Atomic Nazis whirr and click. All through this, the ever present
narrator intones.

NARRATOR

As you watch this film, you are entering a world of horror! We
suggest that you keep your bright lights on as you begin to watch
the terror unfold . . . you will almost be sure that you can hear the
chilling screams . . . the creaking doors . . . the wailing wind . . .
and the other horrible sounds conjured up by the film and your
imagination! You will see wild and sensuous stories of lust and
perversion . . . of horror and the occult . . . madness or realism . . .
believe it or not, you will find this film unlike any other you have
ever seen. Watch carefully, for you know not what lies ahead or
around the corner . . . for you are now entering the world of the
Vampire! BEWARE! Human lust drives men-and women-to feats

of horror they could ill imagine when not possessed by the demon of sexual desire. This film may repel the reader with its bloody picture of passion-crazed people, tormented to madness by the power of their own sexual drives, but it is sure to hold you through to the gory end!

FADE OUT

TV MONITOR.

A video monitor with the evening news fills the frame.

SMIRK WILLIAMS

Brutal slayings in the New Jersey region today as 3 men lay down their lies in defense of the state . . . man in the street Ronald Dobos is there with this report.

EXT. WOODS—DAY

Murder scene, the next day. The police and military prowl about. A wiry, acne-scarred reporter with greasy hair clutches a cheap microphone as a cameraman with a cardboard camera stands by.

RON DOBOS

Uh, Ron Dobos here . . . And it looks like the whole state will be in a world of mourning today due to the tragic deaths of several great men, cut down in the prime of their life. Alan Thicke is dead. I repeat, Alan Thicke is dead.

GENERAL

Get that meddling fool out of here!

Several army thugs beat the crap out of Ron in the background as the detective science boils to the surface.

LT. BROOKS

Well, sir. Looks like this precludes the possibility of any fraud. This is factual data, not fiction.

GENERAL

Oh, shut up. We'll deal with this. We're ARMY, damnit. We don't need that sick old man telling us what to do.

LT. BROOKS

Then . . . it's true . . . the country is being invaded by . . . by horror!

GENERAL

It's true. I never thought it possible. But now . . . the deaths are in front of us.

LT. BROOKS

All blood has been drained from their corpses . . . . I don't know about you, but that spells BADNESS to me. If now you have properly reflected upon the odd disorder of the area, the super-human strength, a ferocity of brutality, a butchery without motive, a grotesque horror absolutely alien from humanity, a voice foreign in tone to all witnesses and a required amount of astounding agility, what results then can we conclude? What impression have I made upon your imagination?

GENERAL

Right. Racist murder bloodheaded bastard death! Well. Not a word to the press about this, we don't want to start a commotion or any sort of panic. And we're NOT consulting that foolish doctor. We will not regress to old housewives! We don't NEED this old character trying to help us. We'll do it ourselves. RIGHT, CORPORAL?

LT. BROOKS

Yehyuhyessir.

Private Popoka waltzes into the room with a phone.

PRIVATE

General, phone call from HQ . . . They want to know what's going on.

GENERAL

Yessir. Everything is A-ok . . . Under control . . . Nope, nothing here is wrong at all . . . there are NO MORE CORPSES. We're dealing with it. Honestly. We don't need any help. Ok, enjoy your time with Chi chi Rodriguez. Goodbye, sir.

Well . . . I'm going to leave . . . I don't see anything.

Doctor Crenshaw can be seen hiding in the bushes. He gasps and walks away.

PRIVATE

Sir, don't you think we should investigate this a little more? Knock around a little and find out what's going on?

GENERAL

No, as far as I'm to be concerned there are no Germans . . . there are no Nazis. Post two soldierly men to guard the place. I don't want senile doctors stumbling around.

LT. BROOKS

I'll get my best men on it right way, sir. I'll also see if they can poke around a bit.. no big investigation or anything . . . just for Security's sake, you see.

GENERAL

Oh, fine. As you wish, corporal. ZOMBIES! PSHAW! NAZIS! HAH!

INT. LAB. NIGHT

Doctor Crenshaw lectures to a snazzily dressed Intoxico while Blue Bastard bites his fingernails in the background.

DOCTOR CRENSHAW

I'm familiar with your successes in combatting the supernatural and the strange, El Intoxico. But weird events are at hand and bad luck is rampant. The power of satanic vengeance is everywhere! Don't you understand? Scienceminded men such as myself have endeavored to delve into this baffling mystery throughout the ages . . .

EL INTOXICO

My friend, this must be some kind of joke.

DOCTOR CRENSHAW

I tell you, dark forces and Nazism is afoot . . . the powers of darkness have united to fight the good that is the forces of good!

EL INTOXICO

Is there danger, Professor?

DOCTOR CRENSHAW

Yes! Brutal desecration and vampiric sufering! There were the damned . . . they looked for the soul searing fires and that is what they received as their reward . . . SOUL! AHAHHA! SOUL? HAHAHHAAH! What is the soul? Can you feel it . . . does it exist . . . can you touch it . . . how do you know it exists if you cannot touch it, feel it, see it. Is it not of the human world if those senses do not exist, then the entity does not exist? I decree this to be fact!

EL INTOXICO
And so I see. This is a most serious matter indeed!
BLUE BASTARD
Right! El Intoxico, this demonic influence is here . . . I've felt
it!
EL INTOXICO
Doctor . . . you say you think the Devil is involved. Mr. Pitch
himself? How can this be so?
DOCTOR CRENSHAW
The Devil will always survive. LIVE is simply EVIL spelled
backward. LIVED then is also simple . . . DEVIL spelled back-
ward. BEWARE! TAKE CARE! Lived searches . . . EVERYWHERE!
EL INTOXICO
Many are already dead due to these unknown horrors . . . 5
men . . . a young girl . . .
DOCTOR CRENSHAW
One so lovely should never die so young. Death is always so
final! So terrifyingly final! So ABSOLUTE!
BLUE BASTARD
Doctor, you say monsters are involved? Vampires? Hombres
Lobo?
DOCTOR CRENSHAW
The animal instinct. The werewolf . . . the monster . . . the
devil himself . . . It was the only emotion they could conjure up in
that instant. There could be no rationality to such a situation. A
fantastic something that craves the living human blood itself!
EL INTOXICO
Yes . . . Yes I see.
DOCTOR CRENSHAW
This monster has . . . the strength of ten men . . . but even ten
men, is a lot less than the power . . . of the drunk man Mexican!
EXT. OUTDOORS—DAY
El Intoxico and Blue Bastard are standing in the middle of
nowhere.
BLUE BASTARD

El Intoxico . . . my friend, I'm concerned with the climate and conditions of this time . . . I fear death is probably nearby!

EL INTOXICO

I say, Brown Bastard . . . when you say more than 4 words at a time . . . I know it is a sign of impending trouble!

BLUE BASTARD

Right! It's a damn good thing we know Monkey Fist Explosion-style wrestling!

EL INTOXICO

Don't worry so much . . . Justice will make itself known!

BLUE BASTARD

Right!

Blue Bastard gestures. WIPE TO:

INT. MARTUCCI'S LAB—NIGHT

Doctor "Oily" Martucci hovers over a sacrificial altar complete with victim. He waves a ridiculous-looking ornamental dagger around.

DOCTOR MARTUCCI

The snake is the god of all the darkness. It is the snake who has enhanced life . . . who might bring into the world all the wickedness we worship . . . and it is to the snake you must extend your soul. Yes! Yes! I will be rewarded! They were selected from elements of the darkness who must do the bidding of the Prince of Darkness . . . his every bidding. Thus is the belief of the witch. Thus is the demand of the devil.

SHIRLEY

You old bastard!

DOCTOR MARTUCCI

I am a lot older than you think . . . I am 140 years old . . . My real name is . . . IRVING FRANQUESTAIN!

SHIRLEY

Then you are.. the man who made . . . el monstro famoso!

DOCTOR MARTUCCI

No. That was my uncle. I'm an altogether different man who does not explore those SPECIFIC arts.

SHIRLEY

An extraordinary monster!

DOCTOR MARTUCCI

Well . . . I admit, I have committed myself to the rediscovery and perfection of that technique . . . using the new blood . . . and the technology of snake-I have determined that golems can be created! SCIENCE-my friend . . . this is the factor . . . the purity of the composite factor of Beta-using it . . . we maintain our youth . . . and live forever!

INT. DRESSING ROOM

Intoxico paces violently back and forth as Blue Bastard puts on a cape.

EL INTOXICO

I can't believe we need to luchar during such a terrible time. A time when injustice reigns!

BLUE BASTARD

El Intoxico, I know that but my friend . . . we are contractually obligated to fight and defend our titles.

EL INTOXICO

Yes . . . but we would better serve mankind out THERE-fighting criminals in all their ghoulish forms!

BLUE BASTARD

Your courage is admirable, but remember my friend . . . we wrestle for the PEOPLE. They need us to grapple . . . it is . . . our burden.

EL INTOXICO

RIGHT!

INT. LAB

DOCTOR MARTUCCI

MUAHAHAHAH! El Intoxico and the Blue Man are in for a substantial surprise during this bout . . . They do not know it . . . but they are about to fight . . . MONSTRUOS!

The camera zooms out clumsily to reveal a gasping Shirley.

DOCTOR MARTUCCI

And then . . . I will transform you into a BEING of superhuman size and consitution! HAW HAW HAW HAW!

SHIRLEY

You fiend! You harrible fiend!

DOCTOR MARTUCCI

Fiend, is it? HA! We shall see how you treat me after that wrestler is . . . DEAD!

SHIRLEY

El Intoxico can never be defeated as long as the alcohol flows in his veins!

DOCTOR MARTUCCI

Well . . . uh . . . we shall soon see!

SHIRLEY

You . . . you sadist!

DOCTOR MARTUCCI

Not sadism . . . SCIENCE!

Doctor Martucci glares and picks up a remote control. He heads for a small tv set with footage of an old Santo bout on it.

DOCTOR MARTUCCI

Don't you see? I've mastered the technology of the future-of control of the libido to resulting of creationisming . . . don't you see? The metric firma supermonster! AH HA HA! Yes . . . yes . . . it will defeat your wrestler on his own ground!

INT. DRESSING ROOM

BLUE BASTARD

Intoxico, I'm worried . . . I've seen your enemy and he looks like a . . . potent brute!

EL INTOXICO

Balloon bastard, you ponder the unmentionables a little too often. Relax, for sadistic wrestling technique will . . . TRIUMPH!

BLUE BASTARD

I guess so, But don't-

Blue Bastard gets cut off in mid sentence.

INT. LAB

DOCTOR MARTUCCI

Yes! For my manbrute monster will be fighting El Intoxico! AHHAAHAHHAHAHAHAHA!

INT. WRESTLING RING

A very cheap monster with a paper bag or equally cheap mask lumbers into frame. The referee gets his throat cut. El Intoxico approaches cautiously and gestures.

EL INTOXICO

Mysterious bastard! You'll pay for doubting my skill . . . I'll defend my exalted title . . . of worldwide drunken kung fu legend!

Monstro doesn't react and kinda stands there. Kinda. Monstro is a little vague. Intoxico is obviously expecting a response and looks baffled. He stares off camera but the crew ignore him.

EL INTOXICO

Fine, then . . . my friend, or should I say . . . most ignoble FOE-prepare yourself to be initiated into my school of ridiculous degenerate MURDER!

Insert another poorly planned "fight sequence" here.

Intoxico is beaten to a pulp as usual and wins at the last minute as the monster is unmasked, revealing a poor rubber mask covered in slime. The monster looks horrified and runs off. Intoxico staggers to his feet and vomits. He falls. Vaguely medical characters carry him out.

INT. LAB

SHIRLEY

El Intoxico! He has shown that once again evil really doesn't understand the situation.

DOCTOR MARTUCCI

Silence! I'll not have you questioning my profound scientific abilties! El Intoxico is DEAD . . . he may have defeated my monstro suuuper, but he has been taken to the hospital . . . OR IS IT THE MORGUE? MUAHAHAHAH!

SHIRLEY

Your perversions of science are unholy! You and your creations will be destroyed!

DOCTOR MARTUCCI

There will never be enough alcoholics to conquer my army of the INSANE! AH AH AHA HHAHA!

Lightning crash. Again.

INT. CHEAP HOSPITAL SET

Intoxico lies in bed. Blue Bastard stands over him

BLUE BASTARD

No . . . no . . . it's not true!

EL INTOXICO

My friend, I'm afraid it is. My spine is broken and they must replace my liver if I'm to take another drink.

BLUE BASTARD

This is tragedy!

EL INTOXICO

Yes, my friend. But please . . . go now to the place of the doctor . . . and . . . BRING FORTH LEWD JUSTICE! My friend, take this radio watch I just invented.

Intoxico produces a cheap wristwatch with a big plastic thing taped to it and hands it ceremoniously to Blue Bastard. Music blares.

BLUE BASTARD

Yes. Thank you, my friend. I will maintain constant communication.

EL INTOXICO

Please do.

BLUE BASTARD

I just want to get close to the face of that IRVING FRANQUESTAIN and turn his bone . . . RIGHT INTO DUST.

EL INTOXICO

His Aryan schemes will be foiled, my friend.

BLUE BASTARD

Right!

Blue Bastard salutes and runs off.

EXT. OUTDOORS—DAY

Blue Bastard waddles down the street accompanied by his stirring theme march.

EXT. MODEL

Model of the castle. Blue Bastard keyed over it. He looks and points.

BLUE BASTARD

I'm coming for you, Doctor! You dictator of murder! Your extortion of goodwill is over!

EXT. OUTSIDE CASTLE

Blue Bastard kicks a door open and enters.

INT. LAB

Blue bastard enters an empty lab . . . He looks at his watch. Superimposed Intoxico appears.

BLUE BASTARD

Come in . . . come in drunkard master. . . . this is el bastard azul llamando con un bulletin de news. I tell you that this lab is indeed here . . . and I see evidence of experimentation!

EL INTOXICO (WATCH)

Right. Keep steady and investigate further . . . I will exit as soon as it is possible . . . my liver is my burden, my friend!

Blue Bastard nods and turns the watch off. He looks around in a padded out investigation sequence, smelling objects and pawing injokey pariphenalia and gimmickry. He occasionally comments on them. Eventually he approaches a table with a sheet over it and after some "suspense" stinking music, the sheet is lifted to reveal a very cheap monster.

Insert fight sequence here. Eventually the mad scientist (clearly not in the same scene and shot earlier) enters the scene and talks to the beaten, chained Blue Bastard.

DOCTOR MARTUCCI

There is nothing a mexican wrestler can do to stop me . . . I hold the secure fate of the un-dead masses and of monstros diabolicos! Because, Blue Bastard . . . there is one thing of an indeed that has been providing me with constant inspiration and metabolic advice . . . that thing is . . .

Martucci lifts a sheet to uncover the LIVING BRAIN OF ADOLF HITLER floating in a mixer or fishtank. Cheap wires and av cables are attached to it. A heavily reverbed german accent squeaks forth in low fi.

HITLER

Tisch! Tisch HEIL! Yes . . . mein Franquestain . . . ju have done the Reich a grand service in creating a monstrous new race of genetic superiors working an advanced control system with orders from the masters in Berlin . . . yes . . . the reich council will be pleased with your results.

DOCTOR MARTUCCI

Thank you, master. Heil Hitler! Don't you see, Blue Bastard? I have the brain of ADOLF HITLER! EL CEREBRO MALO DE UN NAZI ESPECIAL! Mira! Mira! SEIG! SEIG HEIL!

BLUE BASTARD

You bitch bastard! I'll cauterize your fascist ways with my kung fu! El Intoxico will arrive shortly and put a stop to your perverted and illegal methods of race war!

HITLER

SILENCE! National socialism has no agenda that specifies the need or requirement for masked wrestlers, especially those without socialist training . . . you must be enemy, and time for killing death murder is here! SCREAMING BLOODHEADED DEATH!

DOCTOR MARTUCCI

Yes! Yes! AHAAHHA! Don't you see? Aryans dominate the earth . . . and now I dominate alongside the Aryans! Filthy racisms and monsters will join in the hands of linkage business skills and treaty of yes right then PAIN!

HITLER

Quiet! You fool! He's transmitting all this information to el boracho de le mascara . . . . EL INTOXICO!

EL INTOXICO (WATCH)

That's right, you nazi bastard! Don't you think for a moment that as soon as my operation is a success . . . I will revoke your license to practice national socialism in this state! Prepare for maximum penalty of murder!

DOCTOR MARTUCCI

YAAAAAAAAAAAAAAh! Hoooyyyytttt!

Ah-HAH-ha-ha-ho. AH-HAH ha-ha-ho.

Martucci continues cackling in the manner of the "Kung Fu"

stickman character. He punches Blue Bastard several times and tortures him in some horrible way.

INT. HOSPITAL ROOM

Intoxico lies in bed, shaking and screaming.

EL INTOXICO

Aghghhg . . . my liver . . . years of abuse and bending the cells and stressing my tolerances to the breaking point has resulted in a state of crippling injury! That bout killed my will to live . . . and to function . . . because I cannot drink . . . aghghg . . . help me! HELP ME! Oh, spirits of liquor . . .

STOCK FOOTAGE

Operation footage.

NARRATOR

Twelve hours of surgery were required to bring El Intoxico into a state approximating confidence and competence . . . his kung fu skills were at an alltime low . . . but at least his liver began to function . . . soon the drinking would start, and the healing would begin.

INT. HOSPITAL ROOM

Montage of "psyh rehab" training scenes set to peppy music. Inspirational bits of learning how to walk, pushups, crying in slow motion, drinking, etc etc. Eventually he stands up and screams.

EL INTOXICO

My health is back, and my thirsts for the twin perfections fo liquor and brutal murder are back! PRAISE JESUS!

El Intoxico rips off the bathrobe to reveal his traditional suit outfit. He jumps out the window.

EXT. OUTSIDE HOSPITAL

Keyed in pic of a skyscraper. A superimposed miniature intoxico falls. closeup of stock footage intoxico screaming. Stock footage of a dummy hitting the pavement.

EXT. OUTDOORS

Intoxico runs down the street.

EL INTOXICO

I'm coming for you, nazi rapists of culture! Prepare for absolute justice in the style of the old masters!

INT. LAB
DOCTOR MARTUCCI
Ahaahah . . . El Intoxico . . . what a quaint idea . . . a masked wrestler for justice, indeed . . . I hate everything he stands for! But soon he'll be suffering! And I will orgasm in sadistic delight!
HITLER
Yes! Then we will rape women and goats! It'll be revitalizing and rewarding for our productivity, my slave. But first I'll need a vessel . . . a most unholy transport.
DOCTOR MARTUCCI
What do you mean? What on earth could you mean?
HITLER
I demand that you place me inside the skull . . . of the man blue bastard!
DOCTOR MARTUCCI
AHAHAHAHAH!
Zoom into Blue Bastard's horrified eyes.
BLUE BASTARD
Noooo! You'll never get away with this! I'll fight nazism until my dying day! NEVER, do you hear me . . . NEVER!
EXT. OUTDOORS
Intoxico races towards nowhere in particular.
EL INTOXICO
Doctor Martucci, I'll put a stop to your unjust infernal scheming!
INT. LAB
Blue Bastard is now chained to the table as his head is sawed open in a very poor sequence that seems to indicate that the brain of Hitler is being placed within his head. The operation goes on forever, with blinking lights, science sound effects, and sweaty closeups of Doctor Martucci.
DOCTOR MARTUCCI
At last . . . it is done. The man most representative of evil in the entire history of creation . . . is reborn!
Martucci raises his arms and cackles. Stock footage lightning. Martucci flips a switch.

DOCTOR MARTUCCI

And now . . . live . . . live the life of degeneracy and misery! MUAHAAH!

Superimposed electricity crackles over Blue Bastard's body. It breaks the straps and rises. A glowing swastika appears on his forehead.

BLUE NAZI

Nothing in the history of atrocity has prepared mankind for my cruel endeavors!

Abrupt wipe to:

INT. TELEVISION SET

SMIRK WILLIAMS

Bloodshed . . . death . . . depraved lecherous acts of wrongdoing. All of these things are deeply horrible, yet all of these things seem to be happening to the once proud and peaceful land of New Jersey. What can we blame the disruption of our livelyhood on? The answer is simply . . . Hitler. Yes, Hitler. He has taken the very body of Blue Bastard, hero of the land! We go now to Ron Dobos for an in depth report.

EXT. OUTDOORS

Ron Dobos stands with a microphone. He coughs and stares at the camera.

RON DOBOS

Well, Smirk . . . It's true what you say. The whole community is frozen in panic at the deeds this nazi despot is involved in. Nobody ever expected Adolf Hitler to return. But everyone from 6 to 60, from infant to toothless hag can only look to me and mutter softly . . ."Where is El Intoxico?". Where indeed is El Intoxico, idol of the multitudes and drunken hero of the area. Here he is now.

El Intoxico races by the background. Pauses. He walks back into the frame and approaches Ron. Intoxico grabs the microphone.

EL INTOXICO

Hitler! Listen to me as I speak! Are you man enough to face me? I challenge you to a bout to determine which ideology is

appropriate for New Jersey! Hear me now, you filthy bastard! MY
KUNG FU SHALL TRIUMPH!

El Intoxico punctuates his plea by punching Dobos and kick-
ing him several times before trotting off. The camera lingers on a
groaning Dobos before cutting back.

INT. TELEVISION SET

SMIRK WILLIAMS

There you have it. El Intoxico has spoken, but it remains to be
seen whether or not Adolf Hitler will answer and acknowledge his
challenge. Until then, New Jersey will hold it's breath, wondering
if El Intoxico can truly defeat the resurrected Adolf Hitler and his
praeternatural army of complete evil. I for one will be praying.

INT. LAB

Blue Nazi struts back and forth. He knocks a chair over.
Martucci quivers in the background.

DOCTOR MARTUCCI

Master . . . this wrestler will crumble and wither away when
confronted with your bitterness . . . he's nothing . . . I'm confi-
dent in your abilities to defeat him! It's possible, I tell you! You
shall overcome!

BLUE NAZI

I certainly hope this body is adequate! But to insure my
victory . . . we must use trickery and diabolical cunning!

DOCTOR MARTUCCI

Yes . . . yes, I understand . . . but what, Master? What could
we possibly do?

FADE OUT

CHAPTER THREE.

"El Intoxico Contra El Vicio Infernale" (1999)

New Jersey, 1974. A plague of sinister satanic criminals is upon the land, spreading drug addiction and mayhem throughout Monmouth County. Mankind's only hope lies in the sauced brainpan of the Mexican Avatar of Brutality: EL INTOXICO. Summoned to New Jersey by the heavily moustached police commissioner Murray O'Groy, El Intoxico fights the good fight. Repeatedly. Endlessly. Broken bones! Torn ligaments! Maggots! Penis slicing! Hallucinations! Vicious kung fu! Sadistic mobsters! Apemen! A two-fisted French Canadian NAM vet that spouts baffling slang! ALL TRAPPED IN A WORLD OF ENDLESS TORTURE!

EL INTOXICO. The legend. The myth. The cold reality of depravity.

How I envy you. You have yet to experience the bitter realism of it's nasty New Jersey bad breath. 73 minutes of pulse pounding hard edged SLUTTY SCUM await you.

So what exactly are you in for?

Just the most orgasmic film experience of all time. Prepare to twitch for days as your mind plays back each and every harrowing minute of this terrifying motion picture over and over again. On the job. In bed. Driving to work. It will invade your thoughts and steal your soul. But that's the point.

Beyond porn, way the hell away from Hollywood's sterile products . . . El Intoxico is a lust and hate filled romp through the very center of trauma, through the erotic experiences of alcoholism. He conquered his vices by indulging in them, his sexual kung fu was unmatched. El Intoxico: the Mexican manifestation of murder. The modern film that goes ALL THE WAY in exposing the raw realism of contemporary society, bowing before no man or god as it devours our brains.

El Intoxico: you will never forget it. You will never disregard it. There are movies, and THERE ARE MOVIES. This is one of them. Torn from the moldy pages of history, yet soaked in vinegar and updated to appeal to today's troubled teens. EL INTOXICO: the swinging strange world of New Jersey laid bare. EL INTOXICO: nothing is hidden. Every minute is too real, every moment is too much for the immature.

A sweaty exhibition of degradation . . . EVIL beyond comment, beyond description. Have you the courage it takes to withstand the onslaught of TRUTH?

Pleasure, booze, violence. All enclosed within this motion picture. Characters based on police files, characters that shop for sin and take no prisoners. Where does the love start and the deception begin? Can anyone really tell? No, probably not.

Sensational, shocking scandals. See the most twisted depictions of genital destruction. Watch in horror as phallic symbols are ripped to pieces by flamboyant lawbreakers.

Drugs. Chemicals. Kicks. Rugged and rough, the way you like it. Terror! The way you crave it.

Characters. More Characters. People. All of them going somewhere. All of them doing things. We'd like to take this moment to introduce just a few of the piquant personalities you will encounter in this film. Some character descriptions may be the work of G. Groy himself. Be very afraid.

Of course the soul of this film is EL INTOXICO, the bassy dubbed monstrous Mexican wrestler we've all dreamed about. Lord knows I have. Nightly. His burly antics and appetite for liquor will make him a favorite around the holiday season if you allow him into your heart. A keen sense of JUSTICE tempered with violence are among his many attributes.

Gary Groy. A legend among his peers. A filthy degenerate

disguised as an upstanding NJ detective. Gary has lived a hard life, from his time in Eagle Lake battling the bastards of the Allagash, to the sweaty jungles of Vietnam; Groy has taken a lickin'. Mr. Groy has a marked distaste for "gook"; as he calls all foreigners, stemming from his tour of duty and the ninja invasion doesn't sit well with him. Using techniques from his long and torturous upbringing, he dispenses justice the "Biddyam" way. A friend to Intoxico and ally of drunk, breakin' toof and splittin brain in two piece, undisputed 'King of Budweiser', Gary Groy got it going on.

Ninja. Silent killers shrouded in darkness. Masters of stealth. A foreboding legacy of assassination and ruthlessness. These highly skilled warriors have sworn allegiance to no man, until now: The Chairman has recruited the Ninja, and their goals coincide frighteningly. A mission to control all citizens of Mexico and Monmouth County via addiction to extremely potent 'drug'. Their dastardly plan has already been put into effect. It's working better than anyone could have predicted. All opposition to the Ninja has been crushed. There is only one hope. EL INTOXICO!

The Chairman. A babbling retard. An incompetent boob. That is until a highly synthesized 'super drug' made him one of the most cunning and diabolical bastards in human history. The atrocities commited on his behalf are unspeakable, his plans to destroy and corrupt the human race are on a biblical scale, his tactical execution is disturbingly brilliant. Though he has only just begun his reign of terror, many are already calling it the Fourth Reich. No one can equal his brutality, his only fault is underestimating Mexican liquor fighting. Is that enough to topple an Empire?

Murray O'Groy. Brother to Gary Groy. Chief of police for Monmouth County. A man who's world is crumbling around him, Murray has to rely on his perverted brother and a sweaty Mexican to save him. Crippled by ronin in his adopted fatherland of Scotland, he also has a aversion to ninja. A lengthy drug addiction to painkillers almost led Murray O'Groy to the side of The Chairman, yet the pure love of an Apeman saved him. Now he must choose between that love, and the salvation of Monmouth County. Can anyone make a decision like that? Murray O'Groy must.

Johnny Apeman. The heart of this film: loving, compassionate, capable. Born with severe birth defects yet still capable of serving the local police force in an admirable manner. Friend and lover to Murray O'Groy and if you think about it, friend to all mankind. Warm. Kissable. Posseses incredible speed and knows 7 schools of martial arts like the back of his furry hand. We think Johnny Apeman is here to stay and encourage all children to purchase as many Johnny Apeman action figures as possible. Because in the end, what truly matters in life more than a skinny guy talking through a cheap rubber mask in a Thing-Fish voice? If you look into your heart, you'll find the answer is simply . . . Johnny Apeman.

Caifano. Capo di tutti capi. Boss of all bosses: Caifano isn't a player in the rackets, he orchestrates them. Caifano has his hands in everyone's pie and this drug business is right up his alley, but he has no need for middlemen. He is playing the most dangerous game, but his infinite resources allow him to fear no one. A cunning businessman, a concert grade pianist, and a violent brute; Caifano is a force to be reckoned with.

MEMORIES OF EL INTOXICO: the wounds run fairly deep

A mistake? A work of art? A waste of time? The grandest feature in media history? All these things and more. But can we all agree on what exactly took place during the making of this film? No, probably not. What follows are short recollections emailed to me by the cast or trance channeled by G. Groy. Enjoy. Someday I'll set the record straight and give you the full story. Until then, please enjoy the following "entertaining" lies.

JERRY G. GROIN:

I remeber the humble beginnings of Intoxico well.

Andre had come to me with a yet unfinished script and asked me for some input. I read part of it and said "Bah! Mexican wrestling is retarded." That's right. I flatly denied to help script Intoxico. Of course, I regret that now, but I had no idea what a tremendous movie it would come to be. So, Andre finished writing it and he decided to film it. Once again, I took no part in it.

That was until one day he called me and said to come over, he was filming. Ok, what the hell. We had set up a scene to do involving the ninja forcing drug on an innocent. I was to be Intoxico, the role Ian Smith was originally cast to do. We acted it out, all was super and we were done. Eventually, we did a few scenes with me as the Chairman, a role Ian Smith eventually took over. Go figure.

Then disaster struck. Ontor called and told me the news that over $800 worth of film was ruined due to a faulty internal part of the camera. Buttfuckama! And so production on Intoxico was cancelled and it was scrapped. Or so we all thought. Almost a year later, Andre picked up a DV camera and instead of making Rape Lubian bits, Intoxico was given another chance. Even though most would say "That movie is cursed! You're a damn fool to continue that!" We knew better. Digital beats the shit out of analog and production was rolling. Since most of the film stock was a blurry mess of shit, Andre pretty much had to start all over again.

Once again, when he called me to be Gary Groy, I decided I didn't want to do any stupid wrestling movie, and I backed out. Fortunately my piece-of-shitness worked out for the best. I found out later that he had someone else play Gary Groy. Blasphemy! How could anyone else play the Groy? Easily actually. Jim J. Buttocks played him, but not as a french-canadian backwoods brawler. No, as a fucking Scotsman! It is fucking hilarious. Completely bizarre and retarded. Even more retarded and confusing is the fact that I eventually signed back up and played Gary Groy as well. JM J. Buttocks character became Murray O'Groy and the rest is history.

Other than that, the production worked out much better with me on board. After all, I am the whole fucking show. The rest of the production took place in Belmar for the most place. In a slimy stinky drug den. Filled with Belmar people. I really had nothing against them. They were there, had drug, and were willing to act. Good enough for me. The auteur on the other hand hated them

all. He found them to be intellectually lacking. But they have
PLUM! So blah blah blah. We filmed and it was fun and we were
all very drunk and high. In fact, it was a prerequisite for filming, to
drink and drug in perverse amounts. Keep that in my mind while
watching. Also keep in mind that this whole thing is totally false.

DANIEL J. SMITH

I swear I'll tell you about El Intoxico; here you have it. Firstly,
you should know that storms were always brewing, and as a result
my nose ran the entire shoot, which amounted to about five years.
About some of the events that took place during these five years I
will report with whole veracity, leaving out my personal account of
particular matters and only issuing to the reader a sold history of
the El Intoxico production.

The beginning of the shoot was rather confounded as there
were many persons cooped in Andre's basement, smoking noxious
drug and patting their bellies. The devil told the lot of them how
to carry themselves, I'm sure, for no one would give me a ride
home as was promised. Furthermore, I was stifling under their
breath, under which there came many complaints and snores. Yes,
someone was snoring, but who it was I can't remember. I'd guess it
to be Pat, whose last name I never knew, and who at the time
bared a resemblance to Joe Linnette, who was always twirling his
big black mustachio. I tried to tell Joe to quit fumbling around
but he only then showed me his teeth, which I counted.

Not much filming occured during year one: only the scene in
Mexico, New Jersey, where I played a Spanish guitar and Joe
Linnette fell apart. All other film was lost. I tell you I'm sick of
talking about El Intoxico! Regardless, year two-now that I remember there are only two years to the making of this film-involved
Jesse Jason Degrutolla and his wife, who, in the film, were stabbed
in their sleep by a ninja master. It was in year two that Jesse confessed to us that he thought the movie was dumb, and stupid also.
To this, Andre stared pensively with a supercilious brow while he
rubbed his shiny, bald head. "Go to bed, Degrutolla, you're quite
a big baby!"

Caifano then laughed with a cackle as he played a few sour notes on the piano. What was filmed that day was Caifano on the telephone and myself telling Caifano to take a powder. The next night, however, starred Jonny Apeman along with Murray O'Groy. This was only one month before Joe Linnette committed suicide. Luckily within that month Andre taped Murray's last scenes.

And there you have an account of the El Intoxico making, which was almost as arduous and disheartening to create as it was to watch.

ASHISH SHETH:

Dude! Like I am Gashish and Intoxico was the best experience of my LIFE, DUDE! Even though most of my stuff wound up on the cutting room floor; I still think my performance is like the best! D00DZ, let me tell you! I got to work with Groy! He doesn't smell like sour milk and raw hamburger meat, like everyone says he does. More like weed soaked in bourbon. Yo Ho! When we were making this, I was like "Whatever, Go To HE-ella!". Then Andre took me aside and said "Like, we will squirt you with piss." And I'm all like "Yo ho do ho bo ho! Jore k00l. Whatever." Then I saw the finished product and I'm like so happy with it that I show it to all my reggae band members and they're all like DUDE! So if you want to cruise for chicks like Gashish, pick this up dude.

JOHNNY APEMAN:

HOODUM and HEMLO-zem, dere! I am be the Apeman. Johnny Apeman, hemlo. When I'm was approached'm for the role, all my apmens says to the me, "Stupid Apeman! No Apeman can be the act! This'm be the traps'm!" I said "Hooo Hoooo HAAA HAAAAAAA!" and dat scares'm all aways. I must admit though, I was apprehensive at first'mmms. When I go to the set and see all monsters I screamed to me mammy and me pappy. Den a cross-eyed cubano took me aside and said "Eberyting goodsum here." And I say "Hemlooo!" All a suddens, me am be the movie star! Tri-Hoodum! I's am have to be goods, because everyone who see's me in it's gets all quiet and serious'm like. Dat am means I'm good for dem. Hemlo. Now's am be time for me to go'sem. See for yourself.

ɔesman in a Motion Picture'ms. Hoodum. I almost forgets.

h am be an asshole! He beats up on Apeman and has buttsexm's just for the degrades. Hoodum, hoodum, hoodum. HEMLO THERE!

IAN SMITH:

Hi. I play Chairman Leroy Brown. I was the original Intoxico but with a mask, huh, you can't gaze into my undeniable masculinity, and leer at my pubic chin. Andre said I should do it anyway, but I'm so much better than him. I mean how can I take direction from him? Even though he calls himself the director, writer, producer of Intoxico. He's not. I did it all. It's my movie, I just let him take some of the credit because it's not a "real" movie. All he did throughout the picture was rape me of all my ideas. I show the picture every day, even though it's shameful to me. Go figure. I also tell everyone about it, and try to get laid by showing it to people. Be Like Chairman Leroy Brown, tell everyone it's YOUR movie and show it 24 hours a day. Then maybe, just maybe, you can rip your friends off for weed and bad mouth them behind their backs and rape women, and fuck em in the ass just to degrade them. Oh yes, I almost forgot, look for MY movie coming out soon. All I can tell you is that it's a buddy cop movie with Jewish drug dealers. Oh no, now you're going to steal all my ideas. Let me go run and hide inside of a bottle. Oh, and Groy sucks.

An Exclusive Interview with Cinema Legend G. Groy

by Dyquon Foster

To some, El Intoxico was a charming little slice of slightly entertaining trash. To others, it was a revelation. Just who WAS this Gary J. Groy character? You impersonated him for weeks, admit it. His charisma was infectious, his talent undeniable. It was my great pleasure to conduct an interview with this upcoming megalomaniacal recluse.

Q. Children across America are delighted and tickled several shades of inkish by your puckish portrayal of your namesake, Gary J. Groy. But it's also baffling quite a few people. Exactly what does it mean? Who IS Gary Groy?

A. Gary Groy is a cruel perverted bastard that damaged me greatly. He piddles his prick a lot too. Actually, I barely know him. I tried to gain enough information from him to really bring the character home, but, it was hard with him constantly making useless spread sheets and avoiding reality with his laptop. Oh, he's my dad, too.

Q. Why does he talk like that? What's an "allagash cock"?

A. That is a St. John's Valley accent (Northern Maine). As far as the cock thing; you'd have to actually visit the Allagash to know. I don't recommend it though, because they blow up cop cars and set dog's asses on fire up there.

Q. Did you resent Joe Dobos and his "Murray O'Groy" character? I'm told that was supposed to be YOUR part, but you were too drunk and/or lazy to show up that day. Do you think it worked out?

A. That was the "original" part written for Groy. There is a pretty funny story behind that. Ontor called me and said that he was filming that day and I should go. I got drunk instead and said "shit on you, douchebag" and really hoped that I ruined his day of filming. Instead, he got some Jim J. Bullock looking homosexual to do the part. Luckily for me, he was a stupid fucking retard of a butt humper and read the part like a Scotsman. Murray O' Groy sucks ass. Just another Goy wannabe. No wait, it's actually really fucking funny.

Q. Johnny Apeman has been drawing a lot of criticism in the conservative Christian community. Some claim he's a horrible racist cartoon and an affront to all civilized people. What do you think about that?

A. I don't know who the fuck came up with THAT shit! Johnny Apeman . . . a racist cartoon? By my Lord and Savior, Jesus Christ of Nazareth, son of Joeseph and Mary! Never underestimate the power of Hootum. Or tri-hootum or even Hemlo, for that matter. All I can tell is that at least three black negroes of color have seen this film and just watched in fuming silence when Johnny Apeman showed up. Contemplating how amazing his performance is, I'm sure. Next question.

Q. Variety ran an article last year claiming that you were experiencing "creative difficulties" with director Andre Perkowski. Some say his improvisational nontechnique got on your nerves after a while. Can you comment? Were any punches thrown?

A. Completely the contrary, silly bitch. I believe performers should always be given the oppurtunithicity to improvise. I swear by it. That and potent drugs. And very high proof alcohol. And a steady, almost compulsive masturbation ritual. But that's off the record. Eat out more often, as a matter of fact. The only problem I had with the auteur during the production was that he wouldn't pick me up so I could get drunk for my performances. I mean really, would the extra 15 minutes of driving have killed him. My drunken performances are of a much higher caliber. I also had a problem with his editing. I think I could have done better myself. While I realize he's not sitting at an Avid station or anything, come on. Why was I not consulted with any technical aspects of the production!?!? Fucking little sniveling cocksucker. Too insecure to let anyone else try anything. I digress. Oh, as far as any punches. There was a time (on another production)* that he got rather snippy with me. I was going to throw blows to the jaw, to the nose, but I remembered how fragile and weak he had become, due to his constant urine drinking and inactivity.

Q. While some claim this is your first feature, pedantic scholars point to a previous film, "Rape Lube". What can you tell us about that?

A. Just fuck you already. Rape Lube is a very sore wound for me. He really just fucked me over with that one. Fuck you for bringing it up.

Q. Is it true you were used in Devil Girls since Conrad Brooks was too expensive? How was it working on a film and not meeting anyone else involved?

A. Sublimely liberating. And at the same time, nauseatingly oppresssive. Let me elaborate. Being a part time performer and a full time waste of space, I have the obligatory "I'm not doing this good enough. I suck. What the hell am I doing this for?" thoughts.

Doing the Steele character is pretty easy, due to the fact that it's just a voiceover. Should I masturbate now? My monkey is large hemlo dick. Fuck it, I don't care anymore. What the hell do you want from me!?! Is this good enough, oh Grand and Mighty High Lord of everything creative? I'm interested to see how the people who got duped into doing it, and actually invested time and effort, take to such a throw away character. I think it will probably stick out like a sore thumb and be a big black slap in the face to everyone involved. I just like hick. Hick who runs funny!@

Q. A lot of the rumor sites and tabloids are whispering about an upcoming El Intoxico sequel. Can you tell us a little bit about that, or are you sworn to secrecy? Will you be in it?

A. That's just a rumor. I would only take part in that if I were given a little creative control. Not an empirical approach, just more than the original. As far as me being in it? That's really not up to me, is it?

And with that, Mr. Groy punched me in the stomach and fled in his shiny red Camaro. I slowly rose to my feet and realized that this was the greatest day of my life. Wiping away the tears, I smiled to myself . . . knowing that I had just achieved the scoop of the century. And maybe, just maybe, brought JOY with a capital J to Gary's legion of fans. Journalism has its own rewards.

* = Groy is probably talking about the shelved BLOOD CABINET OF DOCTOR MARTUCCI project. Those who have seen the extant 40 minutes or so of it refuse to comment.

@ = Due to computer error and a drunken old man, Conrad Brooks will not be appearing in DG. Gary Groy will not be appearing in DG. So who does? Buy the tape.

Mr. Groy has gone into hiding for several months. Recently our offices recieved this note for him about the "El Intoxico" experience:

Smalltown, USA.

Home of white trash, wife beaters, drunks, vandals, and your run of the mill waste product. Not unlike your town. Very much like mine. Where life seems to sit still unless you're fucked up or in trouble. A barren wasteland of lost hopes and dreams too stupid to care about. This is where I spend my days and live my nights. Like a rat in a glue trap. I lay here, unaware of my eventual lingering death. Or maybe so aware of it, I refuse to acknowledge it. I don't know anymore. And quite possibly, I don't care.

I'm like a wild animal born into captivity. Hand fed each day, never taught how to hunt for my own damn food. No survival skills. Just taught to suckle a plastic nipple, stuck in my face for way too long. I had no idea how hard it could be. No, that's not true. I've seen the other animals released into the wild. Eventually, foresaking their masters for the harsh wild life they were meant for. And I've seen some of them flourish and others ripped apart. Actually believing that I would have to run, and fight for my dinner, never really took hold on my atrophied brain. Reality starts to blur when you view it through TV-poisoned eyes. Fantasies feel more real to me. Though I never try to bring them to life. Sometimes I think I should. Most of the time, I resign myself to the prison of hopelessness and apathy I've created for myself. I'm not asking for your sympathy. It's my own damn fault. I just wish I could fix it. Depression is like quicksand. The more you struggle to get free, the deeper you sink. Eventually, you just lie there, and hope like hell someone will notice you.

Then I starred in 'El Intoxico'.

The end.

Don't let that happen to you. Buy EL INTOXICO right now and count yourself among the living. Thank you.

Liner Notes for Clips:

MASSIVE DRUG ABUSE HEALS ALL WOUNDS: El Intoxico pauses from his crimefighting ordeal to enjoy an odd combination of chemicals that leads to a lengthy hallucination sequence in which he spins around a lot and watches the purty colors. Claymation devils plague him. Featuring the modern sounds of SPIN CYCLE, that loveable teen pop orchestra. Catchy song. We are not responsible for any drug abuse induced by watching this snippet. Do not try this at home, these are trained waste products with years of experience.

WELCOME TO OUR PAIN: The intro sequence and credits to this fine motion picture. Features lots of masks, a brief sequence of horrific "ninja" domination, flag-waving nam vets, and an annoying narrator. Buffed, washed, and spit on to meet your needs. Slutty and inviting. All for you, our very special friends.

THE DEATH OF JOHNNY APEMAN: But can he ever truly die? In this snippet, Mr. Apeman races towards the den of sin only to find a greasy man with pubic chin fuzz. Johnny reacts to the odd facial hair by kinda twitching around. Mr. Pubic then assaults poor Johnny and does some pisspoor kung fu. Finally, Mr. Apeman is shot repeatedly. Sort of. El Intoxico races to the scene . . . too late. Poignant, touching, incompetent: this clip has it all. Bouncy music, too!

EL INTOXICO VS. THE GARDEN STATE: Our favorite wrestler walks from Mexico to NJ only to be set upon by a gang of oily guys in bathrobes in what looks like somebody's backyard. Well, it wasn't my backyard. Nails are thrown. At the time, I didn't have any background music and was sick of the entire "project" so I just randomly tossed in a mystery wav file. Turned out to be a cover of Frank Zappa's "Let's Make the Water Turn Black". Shrug. After this odd little sequence, Intoxico suddenly changes build and beats up some poor teenager behind a Chinese eatery. The place used to be called "Happy Family". You'll be anything but happy after watching this violent clip. Adults only.

EL INTOXICO
CONTRA
EL VICIO INFERNALE
(mexico hero vs. infernal vice)
by andre perkowski
march eleventh
nineteen ninety-nine
draft two
The tender story
of a Mexican Drunkard Wrestler,
and the nation that loathed him.

Ext. Intro Barrage.

Credits roll throughout an intro sequence of ninja brutality. Unrelated examples of extreme violence. A few minutes of horribly cheap looking ninja impaling "normal folk" and throwing nails. You know, doing those ridiculously antisocial acts that only a ninja can do properly.

VOICEOVER:

The year was 1974.

New Jersey was experiencing

one of the most devasting periods

of RELIGION PHILOSOPHY-caused

destruction since the late 19th century.

Using a combination of

devious manipulation

coupled with strong

recruitment methods,

ninja membership was at an all time high.

Aggressive drug sales

techniques were used to

what some would call

an excessive degree . . .

This was New Jersey . . .

Have this over clips of Ninja abuse, ninja forcing strange powders into people faces, injections, the usual gore. Photos or maps of NJ. Also work in shots of the Ninja HQ, the bits with the chairman yelling into a CB radio. Have him bark orders into the CB, and of course hit himself with it repeatedly.

EXT. Crime Scene. Daylight or dusk.

The corpse of a previous ninja brutality is dribbling blood onto the floor. Tie, jacket,sunglass, and moustache-wearing guys poke around and put things in plastic bags. One "detective" wraps saran wrap around his face in a misguided effort to investigate. A camaro pulls up. Detective Gary J. Groy, the chainsmoking french canadian "guy" walks into frame. Smoking. Looking around. Suddenly he yells.

GARY J GROY:
There was fucking
ninja here, man!
I can smell it!
This place fucking
polluted by ninja!
DETECTIVE BOZO:
Well, Mr Groy...
GARY:
Call me Gary or GaryJ,
you fucking tief!
BOZO:
Well, Gary...
it looks like the ninja
struck again for
no apparent reason.
By my count, that's 17 dead.
130 this week.
Grim figures, Gary.
GARY:
Fucking VC prick,
shut the hell up and let me think.
They must've been after something.
The ninja was doin' drug!
BOZO:
(not paying attention, continuing)
Well you see mr Gary,
our stakeout here..
placed earlier
on in the day on
the suspicion that ninja
would be attracted to this landscape...
well, our stakeout . . . uh...
well, they're both dead.
GARY:

Dead from ninja?
You fuck!
BOZO:
Well, these ninja attacks are
just really hurting the economy.
These ninja apparently
have a point
of contention
with the state
of new jersey...
we have to find out why . . . why new jersey...
Bozo continues in this manner, droning monotonously. Groy
suddenly pipes up.
GARY:
I was in Nam you know,
I'm a fuckin veteran. NAM! NAM!
Remember NAM you prick!
I sweat in jungle! NAM!
Continues ranting about Nam while Bozo speaks. Finally he's
interupted by the phone ringing.
Int. Murray O' Groy's Office.
O'GROY:
Gary! Did you catch any ninja?
Heads are going to roll
if those ninja are still breaking laws.
EXT. Crime Scene. Daylight or dusk.
GROY:
No, I didn't get ninja.
Slippery cocksucker ninja
kills all people and run...
They fly, jack.
Int. Murray O' Groy's Office.
O'GROY:
I don't care how fast they fly,
I want them eleminated,

Harold....

EXT. Crime Scene. Daylight or dusk.

GROY:

WHAT YOU MEAN?!!?

FUCKING HA-ROLD, jack?

Dis is fuckin Gary J. Groy, your brother...

fucking blood, man...

But you didn't fucking go to Nam...

Groy continues screaming into the phone until he hits Bozo with it for no reason. He follows this action up by tossing the phone away and suddenly screaming and going into a kung fu pose.

GROY:

KNIFE DISARM KUNG FU!!!!!!

Int. O' Groy's Office.

JOHNNY:

Hemlow.

Dems here ninjasum be

causins da damagums.

Why, justum todaysum

da nin-ja be killins sebenteen men.

GROY:

This ninja is logistically

out of control,

jack.

I want the entire department

working on ninja case...

All available men...

I'll bust that ninja's duff!

JOHNNY:

Hutum.

What I'ms be thinkins

is dat we callsum

da man dey call El Intox-iCO!

O'GROY:

Is your brain working
properly, Johnny?
You callin for the mexican
masked drunk-fight wrestler?
He knows the ways o
fuckin stick-break gung-fu!
THAT STUFF IS DANGEROUS!
Improperly used,
it could result in death
or at least serious injury.
JOHNNY:
Dasright...
He be kickins and
punchsums da ninjasum.
He whats we need.
GROY:
I guess you right,
make call and get
Mexican in office!
INT. El Intoxico's Apartment
Jump cut to establishing shot of a postcard of mexico, sensibly
titled "Meanwhile in Mexico" Cut on over to a filthy hole. The key
word is "filth". El Intoxico is lecturing to a small crowd (w/ straw
hats) on his drunken wrestling techniques.
EL INTOXICO:
(smooth, deep voice dubbed from off-camera)
You see my friends,
the power of drunken
fighting is a privilige
that mustn't be abused.
Channel the alcoholism
and use it for justice.
And then use your ability
for killing of bastard,
but only with a pure heart.

Dude, don't bother me with details.
Dis is Ashish!
O'GROY:
That's it, I've seen enough.
We've got to stop this,
it's . . . it's
unspeakable.
Flagrant abuse of the law . . .
and I'm not going to stand for it.
We need El Intoxico's help!
Where is he?!?!
He should be here by now!
O'GROY marches out of the room.
ASHISH:
Jah, ok . . . .Jou're cool,
whatever . . . go to e-hella.....
Int. O'Groy's Office.
Groy is eating some sort of messy food, getting it all over him-
self. Johnny is pinning little flags to a big map of monmouth county
to see if there's a pattern to these vile ninja attacks
GROY:
Whaddafuck?
It's been 3 days and ninja
out killin' like a
fucking rodney!
Dis Intoxico is nothing
but poppycock...
Pure fabrication...
JOHNNY:
Relaxums,
mista Murray...
dis intoxico is beums commins
from Mexicosum.
He be here's um soon.
GROY:

Well, I hope so...
before ninja kill all fucking baby and people.
     Groy continues eating. El Intoxico barrels into the room
spilling booze. Groy vomits for no apparent reason.
     EL INTOXICO:
     I came as soon as
     I heard about drug.
     These ninja must
     pay the penalty-
     and eat their sins back in pieces!
     MURRAY:
     Stop de ninja!
     Do dis! Johnny!
     Get me some pork chop.
     Johnny scurries off to comply.
     GROY:
     (gesturing)
     Dis map show all place
     where ninja attack.
     It form a shape,
     der is
     a fuckin pattern, man.
     Look here. Dese are
     pictures of ninja.
     Pictures of bastard.
     (obviously still photos over his narration)
     EL INTOXICO:
     I see and
     understand how grave
     your situation is.
     Ninja can be a cruel people
     that show no respect
     for civilized
     society.
     It is up to masked avengers

like ourselves
to police the world and
fight off the ninja.
For the glory of Mexico!
Intoxico gestures. Insert shot of mexicans chanting "FOR THE
GLORY OF MEXICO!".
GROY:
If ninja take monmouth county,
mexico is next. We fuckin
neighbors, jack.
Be on the lookout for hooded prick!
EL INTOXICO:
Right, my friend.
Do not fear
or worry.
I will right the
wrongs and punish
these men for
their indiscretions.
No more will ninja
plague new jersey!
Ext. Window. Daylight.
A ninja at the window observes the meeting and quickly phones
_____, the head evil ninja.
Int. Ninja HQ.
Shabby little HQ with goofy logo on the wall. 2 or 3 bored-
looking ninja slouch around, possibly waving around lit torches
for no discernable reason. The ferociously dull ninja chairman barks
into a telephone.
CHAIRMAN:
Right. I see.
How foolish to send a
mexican to do a man's job.
Right.
(hangs up phone)

Lionel! Get me caifano on the phone!

Ninja #7 peeks into doorway, yells, and runs off. The Chairman injects heroin. After some groaning, he picks up the phone.

Int. Caifano's Office.

Dimly lit "living room". Caifano sits idly typing into a laptop. Random doughy thug leans against a background wall with some crude weapon. Another random thug sits at the table, playing mumblypeg with a series of pencils. Throughout Caifano's conversation, he repeatedly stabs the pencil into his hand.

CAIFANO:

This is Caifano.

Talk to me you son of a bitch!

Int. Ninja HQ.

CHAIRMAN:

Ah yes, Caifano.

My favorate italian.

How are things in the
prostitution business?

Int. Caifano's Office.

CAIFANO:

You never mind that.

Whaddahell do you
want from me?

Int. Ninja HQ.

CHAIRMAN:

There's a certain masked
mexican wrestler in town
that I want dealt with.

I want every bone broken
and every ligament torn.

Please deliver his cartilage
and large intestine
to my office by
tommorow morning.

Int. interior. Caifano's Office.

CAIFANO:

Yeah. I'll take care of it.

I gotta go type notes now.

Int. Ninja HQ.

CHAIRMAN:

Don't fail me, Caifano.

He's a devious mexican that might disrupt our drug trade.

Int. Caifano's Office.

Zoom out from telephone reciever. Caifano is frantically typing notes on a cheap keyboard. He yells a bit.

CAIFANO:

Call the boys and send em out!

I wanna I wanna I wanna!

Horribly out-of-date WIPE on to:

Ext. daylight side of the road.

Intoxico is walking proudly down the street, perhaps saluting passing civilians. Out of nowhere a pickup truck screeches to a halt and an assortment of severely retarded men leap out waving pieces of wood around.

EL INTOXICO:

Cunning devils!

My wrestling ability

will defeat you!

THUG:

Caifano doesn't like you!

Intoxico swigs from a bottle. Inept hand-to-hand combat is engaged. A hick gets a piece of wood impaled in his face. Much bloodshed. Much gesturing. Somehow they subdue him and drag around a dummy with the truck. He eventually overpowers and crucifies the thugs with potent gung-fu. Hmm, one throat-slicing effect . . . one wood impalement in the head.... Punch to the ground death. Vomiting. Blood pouring out of mouth. "Leaves in the face"

EL INTOXICO:

And so you die like the

maggot that you are!

Justice is again maintained!

SCENE NINEBEEE Interior. Bar.

El Intoxico enters and sits down.

Drinking commences. Possible small talk with bartender and "patrons".

EL INTOXICO:

I tell you now,

fighting the criminal element

causes you to come down

with a powerful thirst

for the alcohol.

I must then drown my stomach

with the sauce.

El Intoxico yells various things at everyone. For no real reason a small fight breaks out and Intoxico allows himself some more kung fu extermination time. Perhaps a broken bottle gets stuck in a chest.

*****SCENE 10 interior. Caifano's office

Caifano is on the phone. Random thug clutches his bleeding hand.

CAIFANO:

What do you

mean they're dead?

Fangul! Goddamn mexican!

Yeah. Yeah. Bye.

Caifano slams down the phone.

CAIFANO:

Goddamn wrestler!

Fucking japanese

gonna kill me now!

Caifano clutches pistol and tenses up. The phone rings. Caifano fires. Random thug screams and slumps over.

CAIFANO

AHHHHHHHHH!

Caifano answers the phone.
CHAIRMAN: (v/o)
Caifano. You've failed me.
For this you must die.
Caifano drops reviever. Fires gun wildly.
CAIFANO:
AHHHHHHHH!!!!!
Cheap knife is thrown into caifano's hand. Typical screaming.
Cut to a tv monitor playing a tape of the chairman laughing hysterically shouting.
CHAIRMAN:
GOOD. GOOD.
VERY GOOD.
******SCENE ELEVEN. Interior. Groy's office.
Groy reads memo on clipboard and laughs.
GROY
I was no friend of Cai-fan-oo,
but this ninja business
gotta stop, jack!
I know what this is,
drug is involved.
I was in army,
I know what drug is.
JOHNNY:
Dis be's ans important case.
I gonna be thinkins that I sho
should go downs
to the ninja
and bust dose caps
on dems headsums.
Right on.
Johnny picks up weapon of some kind.
GROY:
You be careful,
wait for El Intoxico.

Fuckin ninja don't
fire blanks. Eclis.
JOHNNY:
I'msgots ta does my part.
For the glory of the poleece.
For my mammy and
pappy, yessir...
I goin ta shows duh ninjas
whats death is.
GROY:
Well, be fuckin careful is what Groy say.
JOHNNY:
Yassir.
And I'ms gonna come back
and brings ya ninja
blood sausage.
GROY:
I hope so, Johhny.
Because you know
how much I love budan.
SCENE TWELVE Interior. Ninja HQ.
CHAIRMAN:
God damn, the ninja are doing good...
good ... very good.
Our competition is eliminated
and the heroin
flows freely
into all the elementary schools.
Our forced addiction program
is going quite well.
(V/O over footage of ninja shoving powder down people's orifi
from the next scene)
AHAHAHAHAHAHHAHA!
(abrubt stop)
RIGHT!

8SCENE THIRTEEN. Outdoors. Anywhere. Daylight.

El Intoxico, walking down the street just happens to pass a mean ninja carelessly forcing drugs on some "guy".

EL INTOXICO:
You hooligans!
By the power of alcohol I
command you to stop
molesting that citizen!
NINJA:
Fuck off, El Intoxico
I need to make a living.
EL INTOXICO:
Inhospitable bastard!
Don't make me . . . hurt you!
NINJA:
I'd like to see...
you try and hurt me!
EL INTOXICO:
Right.
Now I'm going to kill you.

Abrubt standing jump kick directly into ninja. Either trampoline or badly stop motion animated. Ninja screams and spits out much blood. Intoxico approachs the ninja's corpse and tears off the hood. TRUMPET BLAST! It's a hideous zombie!

SWISH PAN TO
Int. Ninja HQ.
CHAIRMAN:
Good, good. Very good.
The ninja zombification
methods have provided us
with an army of atomic zombies,
driven only by a lust for a
blood. Very good!
There will be no stopping my vile
minions of the mangoat!

HAH-HAHhohaho. HAH-HAHhohaho.

HAH-HAHhohaho!

NINJA:

Boss, I don't trust

these zombies.

CHAIRMAN:

Oh, but you must.

Because they are

going to allow

our total domination

of new jersey!

My army of contempt

will rape the land...

VERY GOOD!

NINJA:

Boss, these zombies might turn on us.

CHAIRMAN:

You decrepit

campy bastard!

The atomic zombie

supermen obey me!

I'm the master!

I point the way!

HA HA HA

HA HA!

GET READY FOR TOTAL ATOMIC

NINJA ANNIHILATION!

Ah-HA ah ah ha ha haw!

INT. SEEDY BEDROOM

El Intoxico relaxing at home in normal pants and an unbutton

shirt. The phone rings.

EL INTOXICO

Habla El Intoxico..

que tu quieres?

GARY J GROY

Listen up, jack . . .
the fight tonight,
man . . . it could be rigged . . .
I suspect that CAI-Fun-o
is involved.
EL INTOXICO
Yes, my friend. I will
take heed of your warning.
And in this bout of mine . . .
I will do what is right.
Right for Mexico, and
right for it's people.
GARY J GROY
Right . . . my friend . . .
in Nam . . . you would have
been appreciated!
EXT. Roads or Hoboken.
Johnny Apeman races through the streets or suburbs in a spastic
manner, accompanied by ridiculously inappropriate music.
Int. Ninja HQ.
LIONEL:
(mincing assistant ninja speaks up, maybe staring into a
monitor. Cutaway to footage of Apeman running)
Boss, what looks like an
ape is approaching.
He looks like trouble.
CHAIRMAN:
Right.
Go on and send out
some of the zombie-
ninja to take car
of this little ape.
Zoom in to his eyes. Dramatic chord. Awkward pause.
CHAIRMAN:
(nintendo kung fu laugh over and over again)

AH-HA—HA . . . HA . . . HA!

Ext. Ninja HQ building.

Two ninja stand outside with torches lit. Johnny Apeman walks up.

NINJA #1:

We said nobody can come so

nobody's going to come.

NINJA #2:

They never said somebody

was going to come so nobody's

going to come.

NINJA #1:

Somebody's going to come but no

because nobody is

going to come.

NINJA #2:

Right, we can't allow anyone to come.

Nobody is

allowed to come.

NINJA #1:

No police here.

Apeman suddenly lunges and defuses the two ninja with moderate gung fu. Johnny cuts them up to make blood sausage. Apeman brushes himself off and enters the building.

Int. Bar.

El Intoxico continues to drink. Murray O' Groy enters. O' Groy drinks.

O' GROY:

El Intoxico!

What are you doing here?

EL INTOXICO:

Honing my drunken-

fighting skills

by continuous practice.

To maintain my peak

effeciency, I must pound
down the drinks and knock
back the booze continuously . . .
otherwise . . . one small mistep . . .
and it would be . . . ALL OVER!
O' GROY:
That's all well and good,
but Johnny went to fight
those damn ninja...
BY HIMSELF!
EL INTOXICO:
My friend,
He'll be torn apart!
His kung fu isn't anywhere
near good enough!
It's weak! He has good intenions . . .
and a good heart . . . but
his kung fu leaves
much to be desired.
O'GROY:
You've got to
help him! You must
save Johnny apeman!
EL INTOXICO:
RIGHT!
O'GROY:
You've GOT to help him!
Because you see . . . he's
not only my partner...
But . . . El Intoxico,
he's my . . . my lover.
EL INTOXICO:
I understand the love you share.
O'GROY:
It's

a deep love . . .
a mutual bond . . .
I look into his eyes, and see
a reflection of myself.
Ape love is a difficult thing to understand, Intoxico.
EL INTOXICO:
I understand perfectly,
Mr. O'Groy . . . I
was in love once . . .
to an Apeman . . .
It ended badly,
but I'll never forget him . . .
I'll never forget what he did to me . . .
That summer . . .
that magical summer when he taught
me what it was
like to be a man . . .
and I taught it
him the true meaning
of being an Apeman. The
things he did to please . . .
O'GROY:
Yes . . . yes, it's touching.
so save him . . . Save my Johnny Apeman.
And..
And just in case,
I gave my brother Gary J O'Groy a call.
His kung fu is very good indeed.
EL INTOXICO:
The french canadian kung
fu is regarded in some
circles as the finest kung fu.
I welcome your brother's assistance in
ending this ninja plague . . .
this sticky threat

that all honest men
hate with all their hearts . . .
I hate the ninja . . .
what they have done
is inexcusable . . .
the narcotic
drugs they sell . . . are
impure and dangerous to
those who strive to be correct . . .
those who strive to fight for
justice . . . those who would like to make a
difference. The ninja are an
obstacle to all god fearing
citizens and all mexicans . . .
indeed, all men who would
fight to keep humanity pure.
(Intoxico goes on a long long long rant about nothing in particular while O'Groy purchases booze from the bartender and gives
it to that charming masked wrestler.)
O'GROY:
You're going to need this to
boost your strength, m'lad.
Only permanent liver damage
can save you now!
But liver damage that is not
just a curse . . . but a blessing!
EL INTOXICO:
In this reasoning
you are correct.
Now, I must be off to the
devious ninja headquarters
to pound the fear
of Yahweh into them.
O' Groy:
Remember to bring back some

blood sausage for my family.
EL INTOXICO:
(while racing off)
RIGHT!
Ext. daylight road
More bits of Intoxico-running-down-the-street-drinking
footage. A ninja on a roof watches him.
EL INTOXICO:
(calm v/o)
I had to reach the ninja filth-hole soon,
if I intended to save Johnny
from a slow, painful death.
Did he deserve to die?
Was there some crime in him?
Have I drank enough?
El Intoxico kneels down to pray.
EL INTOXICO:
I beseech thee and
worship all gods of liquor.
Alcoholic spirits, hear my call.
Let me gain the
courage of drinking
and the knowledge of
brutal alcoholism.
For mexico's glory and
until the armageddon!
ALCOHOL!
A superimposed very silly "old god" face is superimposed over
his plea.
DEUS EX ALCOHOLICA:
(booming, heavily reverbed voice)
ELLLLLLL INTOXICOOOOOOOOOOOO!
EL INTOXICO:
I feel myself replenshed
with the energy

of generations
of drunkards.
My wrestling skills
are at their peak
and I feel I'm ready to
take on Pitch himself.
Yah!

Intoxico swills more liquor. The Ninja fires a rifle from the roof and attacks. Much violence and yelling ensues. Pow bash biff hurt yell. They scream the name of their techniques before attacking, as per the usual kung fuhell. The ninja runs away.

EL INTOXICO:
RICKMAN! RICMAAANNN!
I Know it was you!
San Felipe, 1984.
I never forget a face!
RICKKKMAAAAN!
INT. NINJA HQ.
CHAIRMAN:
Stupid idiot!
Defeated by that masked man!
NINJA:
But, Boss. He's a good wrestler.
CHAIRMAN:
I don't care if he's
Leaping Lanny Popoff!
If you fail
me again,
I'll kill you and
make you a zombie!
You'll be dead like the rest!
NINJA:
Sorry, Boss.
It must be my reactive mind.
CHAIRMAN:

Your reactive
mind is going
to get you into a lot
of trouble someday...
Xenu isn't going to appreciate it...
NINJA:
I don't want to offend you, boss...
But.. You're crazy!
CHAIRMAN:
That might be the case...
But my insanity is
perfect, like a diamond.
Like a very good
diamond . . . very good....
My insanity is
completed and
perfected . . . refracted from
the crystal and instensified
by the teachings of Elron . . .
You can't
understand me.
You can't comprehend my awesome power!
Crazy? Ha!
If only it were so
simple . . . but I suppose
to the simple . . .
such as yourself.. IT IS!
NINJA:
I'm sorry, boss.
I . . . I'm trying . . .
I just can't
believe in-
CHAIRMAN:
You can't? You can't . . .
You've been

deluding yourself . . .

for this . . . you must die.

The chairman calmly opens a draw and takes out a long spiky blade.

NINJA:

Boss . . . please don't . . .

I've been a loyal servant of

your organization

for years . . .

please . . . my children . . . Umberto

and Amos . . . what

about them?

I . . . I . . . boss . . . please . . .

CHAIRMAN:

No, Ralph . . .

for you there is

no salvation . . .

or perhaps there is.

Perhaps in death,

you will realize

and learn from

your mistakes.

I hope this will be the case.

NINJA:

Boss . . .

please . . . I . . .

CHAIRMAN:

Your first mistake . . .

will b

your last.

Enjoy the death of the

dead! YAAAAAH!

The Chairman plunges the large metal spike into the Ninja's head. Our poor Ninja flops around screaming. He tugs at the blade. The Chairman cackles and smears his hands with blood.

CHAIRMAN:
Death! Death!
It pleases me!
The blood of the living
is my only sustenence!
Oh, Dark Lord Gorto . . .
be kind to thy servant!
For I shall be kind to
the dead! And unto you!
Hark ye herald angels sing,
Glory to ME!!!
HAHAHAHAHA!
Int. Ninja HQ.
LIONEL:
Boss, our men are dead.
And El Intoxico is
here to visit.
CHAIRMAN:
No problem.
Send out some ninja
while I sacrifice
someone to Satan
to gain demonic
wrestling power!

At this point it goes into a Sho Kosugi elaborate "suiting-up, doing bad tai-chi" nonsense set to overblown soundtrack music.

Ext. Daylight.. Ninja HQ Building.

Intoxico arrives on the scene and quickly examines the unconscious ninja. He kicks one for entertainment . The body moans and vomits blood.

EL INTOXICO:
Disgusting bastard!
GARY J GROY:
(appears out of nowhere waving pistol around)

Hold the fuck
up, jack.
EL INTOXICO:
(turns around, gestures yet again)
Who in the nine
hells are you?
GARY:
Eclis, man.
Dis is Gary . Groy…
I' m with poe-lice.
EL INTOXICO:
Is that so?
I'm mightily impressed.
GARY:
I better fuckin' go wit you to kill
Eagle Lake
Ninja before
Fort Kent is surrounded.
EL INTOXICO:
Well. My friend. Right.
Yes! Well, be
you careful is what I suggest.
Thank you, then.
Ext. Outside Ninja HQ.
Groy and Intoxico cautiously look. 2 Ninja jump in out of
nowhere and do bad kung fu. Someone, possibly Groy . . . vomits.
Fighting. Etc. Etc.
GARY J. GROY:
Vietnam taught
me wall, jack.
Knife-disarm kung fu
work like a charm…
EL INTOXICO:
I understand,
but I must tell you that

alcohol increases
fighting comprehension.
GROY:
Waitaminute, man.
Dis fucking
Ninja is something else...
I know what this is...
Groy rips off ninja hood to reveal a bad zombie effect.
GROY:
Dis is zombie!
EL INTOXICO:
Yes of course
I know this,
my friend.
I just didn't want
to get you alarmed...
Now, we need to
figure out a way in...
INT. LOCKER ROOM
El intoxico is preparing for a bout all of the sudden, in a
jumpcut that leaves you wondering. Groy walks into the
scene . . .
GROY
In this fight now . . .
you could be fighting
with TEEF!
In league with DEV-
IL . . . Intoxico.. be careful . . .
EL INTOXICO
Tu sabe que yo siempre
tengo cuidado.
But I tell you that I know see
things from another
world . . . I see
clear entities warning

me of the danger.

INT. WRESTLING RING

Intoxico takes time off from the movie to wrestle . . . lots of padding, and sped up footage of a bout set to stock footage crowd noises and STOCK CROWDS, nobody is in the background. Keep cutting to someone seated in the crowd giving the evil eye accompanied by sound effects . . . Something happens in the ring, the other wrassler unmasks and the fight turns deadly, as usual. The other wrestler wears a bad rubber mask and El Intoxico continues to grapple with it. The bout doesn't stop, but El Intoxico triumphs of course. The bell rings and El Intoxico drinks heartily.

EL INTOXICO
Mexican brutality is the
purest, most honest
brutality!
Int. Ninja HQ.
LIONEL:
That goddamn whore-bastard.
Boss, his kung fu is good.
We didn't
count on that . . .
He even managed
to stop our zombies!
I've never seen
such destruction!
CHAIRMAN:
Well of course his kung
fu is good-
he's mexican!
What did you expect?
LIONEL:
Boss, I think we should run
away right now.
Right?

CHAIRMAN:
You cowardly BASTARD!
The ninja never run.
LIONEL:
Boss, I think that
strategically speaking,
it's our best option.
CHAIRMAN:
(watching El Intoxico fighting footage on a small monitor)
Well, I suppose
you're right.
Get the jet ready.
LIONEL:
Right boss.
Just come this way.
Int. Miniature Hell
GI Joe plane "flying".
CHAIRMAN(vo)
I doubt there's
a mexican alive
that can stop a
jetplane in midair.
That bastard is going to
pay for all this...

The ninja attempt to escape in the plane. Cut to cheesy jet interior. El Intoxico races outside the building and throws a rope on the jet, pulling it back to earth. The ninja eject without parachutes and just leap down.

SCENE TWENTY-TWO: FINAL FIGHT HOLOCAUST MORTAL BODY BLOW HOLDS BARRED

Trampolines used excessively. Fighting fighting and more fighting While Intoxico handles Lionel, a ninja seemingly Groy. REVENGE FOR YOU

SCENE TWENTY-THETHREE
Int. Shitty, filthy bedroom.

Intoxico is sprawled on the bed smoking the foul weed with roots in hell and eating hot pockets (maybe show him microwaving them in the kitchen as well). He's watching Dolemite or any Rudy Ray film. Suddenly Gary Groy bursts in.

GARY GROY:
Intoxico!
What the fuck you
doing smoking drug
and eating da hotpocket?
You fucking lazy bastard...

EL INTOXICO:
My friend,
I need some time to recuperate
between wrestling matches. I find that
in times like this,
the devil's weed is an
appropriate weed. I feel
calmed, as if I were in a state
that would
approximate
peace . . . in this peace, I find
understanding,
and by understanding,
the reasoning
process is completed . . .
Yes, I'm glad. Very glad.

GARY:
Get fuckin going, jack!
Ninja are out there! Everywhere!
Be careful around fucking Ninja,
they smart!

EL INTOXICO:
My excitable policeman friend,
I suppose you are right.
Just give me a minute to

get going and prepare
for that which awaits me.

Intoxico "does" a nitrous cannister whilst Gary J. Groy yells in
the background.

GARY:
Hurry up, you prick-bastard!
They in a car driving
fast like bastard!
I saw him! In a car . . .
that way!
It fast, jack . . .
speeding!
INTOXICO:
Yes, I understand.
This breach
of the law in regards to the speed
limit is one in which I am
not at my utmost level of comfort . . .
I see now how serious
this situation is.
However . . .
The drug's hold
is great...
I need to gain strength.
Intoxico drinks heavily. Gestures.
INTOXICO:
And now at last
I have the power
of burning hot booze within me.
The alcohol flows
through my bloodstream!
It energizes . . .
it revitalizes . . .
my blood . . .
is replaced . . .

WITH LIQUOR!

Intoxico screams, destroys a vase or something, and races out of the room.

GARY:

Mexicans.

Fucking Mexicans.

CRAZY!

EXT. STREET—DAY

El Intoxico runs at top speed down the center of a highway, screaming the entire time.

NARRATOR:

El Intoxico...

the man who could drink

a thousands drinks.

The most famous and honored

man in mexico,

a man who could kill ninja

in his sleep.

The greatest wrestler

of his time.

El Intoxico can run up to 80

kilometers an hour,

achieving even more if

he's been drinking.

He's chasing after a car seemingly going quite fast. Intoxico speeds up.

EL INTOXICO:

Hold now!

Stop, I say!

I command your motor

vehicle to come to

a complete halt!

I request, in a formal way,

that your

automobile please

pull over to the side of the rode!

INT. CAR—NIGHT

It's suddenly switches to night. The Chairman is in the back seat. Several ninja accompany him. The Chairman turns and watches Intoxico for a moment.

CHAIRMAN:

That wrestler . . .

he runs as if possessed

by the forces of good . . .

I'm impressed,

but not so impressed

that I don't think . . .

I'll WIN!

NINJA:

Boss,

what will we do?

He seems to know

all the tricks . . .

his grace . . .

his stamina . . .

his acting is

impeccable!

The way he delivers dialogue . . .

NINJA #2:

We're lost!

We're lost!

Judgement day is upon is!

El Intoxico knows of our

essential impurity

and inner evil!

He will kill us

repeatedly . . .

his mexican wrath will

not be escaped!

I know this in my heart to be true!

CHAIRMAN:
Shut up, you simpleton.
There is ALWAYS a way out
of such
scenarios . . .
We have the upper
hand . . .
There is a way . . .
I have
a plan . . .
Driver!
STOP THE CAR!
EXT. STREETS
The Ninja car screeches to a halt. A door flies open. The Chairman tosses a Ninja out the window. A blatant dummy flies through the air.
CHAIRMAN:
Distract him!
The Chairman, grabbing another Ninja by the scruff of the neck, gets out of the car and trots towards the dirt. Meanwhile, the other Ninja engages Intoxico in a little brawl.
EL INTOXICO:
Prepare yourself for
spiritual oblivion!
The suffering I will
impose on your body
will be one that you cannot
stop or ignore!
El Intoxico starts beating the crap out of the Ninja. Eventually he's just tossing the dummy around and punching it's head repeatedly.
Meanwhile, the Chairman pulls out a knife and scratches a pentagram and some ridiculous symbols into the dirt.
NINJA:
Boss, what are you doing?

That looks . . . unclean . . .
diabolical, yet
oddly compelling.
CHAIRMAN:
What am I doing, you ask? Well . . .

The Chairman plunges a knife into the Ninja's heart and tosses him into the center of the pentagram. He pulls out a torch from nowhere and lights the Ninja on fire.

CHAIRMAN:
Oh Mighty Dark Lord Gorto,
he who watches over us all . . .
please give me the means
to defeat
El Intoxico..
I present you with this gift,
a fine soul and member
of my organization..
his death is one that
will please you..
Oh, Gorto . . .
I beg of
thee . . .
Help me in this
time of tribulation
and trouble!

Through a series of terrible special effects, a hideous apparition appears floating over the fire.

GORTO:
Good hello, my servant.
I trust you are well.
I accept your sacrifice,
it pleases me greatly.
Please accept my contrib-
ution to your cause . . .
A fiend from HELL!

CHAIRMAN:
yes . . . yes this will
please me quite well!
A fiend from Hell can
stop a fiend from Mexico
without much of a fuss!
GORTO:
AHAHAH! Sputter mutter,
everyone wants
to kill this Mexican!
CHAIRMAN:
What?
GORTO:
Forget it. It's an injoke.
Anyway,
here's the fiend.
Hope it works out for you.
Let me know
if you need
anything else,
Donald.
Kiss.
Gorto dissapears. The flaming ninja corpse starts to glow. It's
filled with zesty, tangy satanic energy. It slowly moves up. A whine
fills the soundtrack.
CHAIRMAN:
It's working . . .
it's working . . .
The powers of hell
are on my side!
Praise Gorto!
Meanwhile, Intoxico kills that Ninja/Dummy. He looks up at
the transformation.
EL INTOXICO:
AHHHHHHHHHHHHHHHHHHHHHHH!

Noooooo! It can't be!
Pope John Paul, please give
me the courage and intensity
to destroy this creature!
Help me in my moment of need!
Help me the way I've helped you . . .
the way I've helped the people!
El Intoxico looks up at the sky and strikes a dramatic pose.
Pause. Nothing happens.
CHAIRMAN:
Your precious Pope
can't help you know,
Intoxico!
Face it, it's over!
EL INTOXICO:
As long as the sperm of Justice
fills my testicles,
I will never give up hope . . . . DIE!
Meanwhile the hellfiend critter bubbles, stopmotion animates
around, continues glowing. He mutates a bit and turns into a
rubbery, slimy creature of some sort. Oh, and the sky turns red for
no real reason for this segment. El Intoxico rushes towards the
creature. Right as he's about to reach it, the Chairman sticks a foot
out, whistles innocently, and trips Intoxico. Intoxico falls in slow
motion and collapses into a heap directly in front of the hellfiend.
The hellfiend drools. Pause. The Hellfiend grabs Intoxico's head
and bites down. HARD. Blood sprays everywhere. A chunk of
brain is exposed. The hellfiend spits out clumps of tissue and more
blood. The Hellfiend crumples to the ground and dissolves.
The Chairman cackles.
CHAIRMAN:
YES . . . YES . . .
It is done!
I knew Gorto would never fail me!
I bet you expected a climactic

fight sequence . . .
you against Hell . . .
well Intoxico, I'm
very sorry you were cheated . . .
I had to cheat . . .
and now you're
cheated . . . OF A LIFE!
HAHAHAHAHAHAHA!
I'll see you in Hell,
Intoxico!
EL INTOXICO:
URHGGGGGGGGGGGGG!
El Intoxico shuffles towards the Chairman. His eyes now glow.
Intoxico is apparently a braineating zombie.
CHAIRMAN:
Well, it's been a pleasant
little excurcion,
Intoxico.
I hope you've enjoyed
it as much as I have . . .
but, you're a busy man . . .
So I think I'll exit stage right . . .
See you around, dear.
The Chairman casually gets back into his car and drives off.
Intoxico groans and stumbles down the street.
EL INTOXICO: (reverbed voiceover)
I . . . I . . . no . . .
this couldn't be . . .
My entire life . . . over . . .
I had become . . .
a hellfiend myself . . .
a soulless creature filled with . . .
filled with hell . . .
I had no reference points
for my present situation . . .

How could I deal with it?
What would become of me?
Will the children
respect me if I serve Satanic forces?
I . . . It's over . . .
isn't it . . . a life dedicated
to Justice and
controlled by liquor . . .
a pristine life . . .
it's over . . . My life . . .
My livelyhood . . .
But, fate had dealt me a cruel,
unforgiving hand.
It wasn't exactly over . . .
not in the way it usually
is when people die . . .
I wasn't decomposing
in a grave . . .
I was decomposing
as I moved around . . . .
Fate . . . blind fate . . .
where had I failed?
Where have I gone wrong?
Did I truly deserve this?

Intoxico continues walking down the street. Generic citizens scream and run off. Intoxco passes an old blind man in a lawn chair. Though blind, the old man is flipping through some sort of porn magazine.

EL INTOXICO:
He doesn't know..
the man can't see me . . .
if he did, he would go mad . . .
I was a walking horror,
a living testament to the
cunning of evil . . .

Ordinarily,
I would engage this man in
friendly conversation.
Today was different.
I'm different now.
I need to accept this
if I'm to make progress.
OLD MAN:
Who's there?
Who . . . I hear you . . .
LEAVE MY MAGAZINES ALONE!
I bought them for my enjoyment!
Leave an old man alone!
EL INTOXICO:
I knew what I must do.
The time had come and
I wasn't one to
keep time waiting.
I never was.
And I'm not about to start.

Intoxico takes a bite out of the old man. Blood spurts every-where yet again. Intoxico tears the old man's eyes out and bites an ear off. Screams.

He chases after the ninja. Final battle. The ninja reveals him-self to be Groy. Much death ensues. ! Bluescreened final battle-silly anime "hyperspace" lines chromakeyed in. Explosion footage Horrible injury is the final result .

Intoxico burns himself alive. Citizens ponder the meaning of existence and the drunken wrestler up in the sky watching us all. His image is dissolved in slowly. Mexican music swells. Roll credits and outtakes.

RECYCLED IDEAS AND
INTOXICATED INTOXICO FRAGMENTS FROM THE
YEAR 19 THE 98 and 99
for the FINE SEQUEL

Titles appearing and describing his moves:

Seven Golden Dung Beetle Air Conditioner Dragon Fist Style Kung Fu

Brown Vest Monkey Fist Explosion Fu

After a car chase, the ninja "leader" while running ponders whether or not he should sacrifice someone to satan for help. He does. The infernal wrestling match kills intoxico, turning him into an undead wrestler who needs to eat human flesh to stay alive.

Throw one of those bluescreen segments during the mexico scene.

El Intoxico and Blue Bastard vs. The Vampire Women and El Hombre Lobo.

Blue bastard wears a turtleneck and the brown jacket.

that I do with more color unless it's the horror parts.

Walking around red bank. El Intoxico and Blue Bastard.

Some oily guy summoning the vampire woman and her wolfy henchman.

Toight the blood from the anti-christs will flow, and give rise to the ultimate horror!

Joe as the grey-haired, pipesmoking professor in a good suit. He pontificates.

Steal the atomic zombie stuff I wrote for this. A mad nazi doctor revives them. Good, that gives me some extra pages to play with.

I'm familiar with your successes in combatting the supernatural and the strange, El Intoxico. But weird events are at hand and bad luck is rampant. The power of satanic vengeance is everywhere! Don't you understand?

My friend, this must be some kind of joke.

I tell you, dark forces and Nazism is afoot . . . the powers of darkness have united to fight the good that is the forces of good!

Is their danger, Professor?

Yes! Brutal desecration and vampiric sufering!

El Santo's origin myth.

brief groy appearance.

degrutolla wolfman footage.

budan.

female "ninja" segment

Bob Dole

all the carter apeman stuff

most of the chromakey stuff.

WWII footage padding things out . . . bits of hitler and stuff taped off of TV.

Pipe smoking professor . . . lots of voiceovers reading pages and pages of nonsense with diagrams and stupidity. stooock footage. pacing back and forth. talking to the wrestlers. eventually he's killed by either the vampire woman or the wolfman.

use that wooden thing in the garage with some "additions" as a cheap coffin.

Rex Adamson, EL HOMBRE LOBO.

Throbbing Vomit Punch Kung Fu

Intoxico drinking too much during a battle. Much throwing up. So he fails. Gary Groy dies, or appears to. Silly screaming "REVENGE FOR YOU"

MORE intro scenes of ninja attacks on the population. Have O'Groy try to deal with the problem himself . . ."investigating" the "crime scene" . . . ah! So they call in Larry Wu to do the scene with the coffee spilling...

Hmm, the scott footagee can be him telling O'groy the fact that the ape is dead. Cut to silly "dream" sequence of O' Groy screaming "Johnny", them running in a field arm in arm, etc. Cut back to O'groy sobbing hysterically. He then kills himself either by rifle or wrist-slitting. Or both. He could fail at shooting himself...

The ninja manage to inject El Intoxico with nameless "Drug". He goes on a wild hallucinatory rampage, claymation horrors everywhere, masks, etc etc. He finally manages to counter the effects through the power of drinking.

Ninja sends a woman (he hypnotizes her with christmas lights on his mask) to seduce el intoxico, she gives him a hallucinogenic brew. Goes on rampage. Kills.

Ninja sacrifices a girl to satan to help him defeat el intoxico. A demon wrestler appears. Fights Intoxico in an infernal wrestling ring.

Eye gouging.

Ninja removes his mask and he's Gary Groy.

Crime scene intro. Groy AND Groy investigating. I know what this is . . . this is drug. Ninja drug."

"The chief is leaving"

Intoxico drinks and breaths fire.

El intoxico is a masochist. Women whip him.

He becomes a pothead in the middle of the movie, sits around watching shitty movies while eating hot pockets. Then a groy pours booze down his throat so he snaps out of it.

Dual unmasking during the final fight.

Tobewritten:

Ninja hypnotizing woman with christmas tree lights

Woman seducing Intoxico

Bedroom: partial nudity, Intoxico takes drugs.

Intoxico Freakout deathrampage hallucinogenic hell

Ninja considering a sacrifice to help in his intoxico crusade

Ninja satanic sacrifice. Satan appears.

El Intoxico is sent to hell by bad special effects

Intoxico vs Stupid Demon in an infernal wrestling match.

O'Groy in his office sobbing and reminescing about johnny. He kills himself.

Intoxico becomes a pothead and sits around. O'Groy gets him going.

Gary Groy killing someoen with a star or throwing knife, for no real reason.

Horribly mismatched day and night shots

Boring science talk-gack, the ninja are zombies of course.

When they remove their hoods, blue makeup, circles under the eyes, theatrical–looking and silly . . . latex clumps randomly applied . . . PERFECT, Intoxico can remove the hood, a trumpet blasts and it zooms in.

Chairman goes off into a long villanous tirade concerning nothing in particular ending with the overzealous evil man knocking over a bunch of equipment or possibly punching out the assistant ninja.

The long hallucination sequence will be perfect . . . Starting with subtle distortion and flo-motion, then color offsetting insanely, kaleidescopic intoxico heads screaming, claymation horrors bluescreened in. . . . Menacing guys in masks running around (use up the rest of the mask reserve for this-they all make cameos . . . Looped Murray O' Groy admonitions superimposed on top of Intoxico gasping and pawing at his face. Eventually he imagines he's running through a field on his hands and knees...the sky changes colors and the glow effect is used plenty of times-In fact this would be a good way to pad out 8-10 minutes with an incredibly long nonsensically surreal intermission about 40 minutes into the movie . . . Definetly before the "final onslaught" of the HQ.

Incorporate more spanish/mexican things into Intoxico . . . stock footage of Mexico, and also the LANGUAGE.

El Intoxico needs a meaningless roman catholic priest to quote scripture and drool.

He slows down the investigations and just rambles with the police in long, talky scenes.

THE YEAR OF GRACE.
El Caballero
de plata
Este hombre es un mexicano importante!
El mascaro de la botella . . . en esta ano de gracia,
el intoxico . . .
Hairdo . . . pompous . . . weird.
This movie is fucking alien.
What's happening, Intoxico?
If I told you . . . you wouldn't believe me.
Oh, why is that?
It doesn't matter . . . I'm GOING TO KILL YOU!

———

Tonight, the masked mexican drunkard . . . WILL BE DEAD!

cut to ANOTHER bout. In the middle of another scene, seemingly before Intoxico finishes a sentence, he's suddenly in ANOTHER bout, blatant recycled footage with the same crowds, a different enemy, and a brutal turn: make a horribly GRUESOME end to this bout . . . castration and intestine chewing, beatings with a chair, constant WRESTLING.

Intoxico scares away the forces of SATAN constantly, with a big crucifix . . . he fights crime, he defends mexico, fights MR. PITCH . . . everyone, really. That's INTOXICO for you.

El Intoxico goes to help . . . red tinted footage, loud sound effects, moans and people yelling. He goes to get Johnny Apeman back from satan or something.

Office . . . the general . . . a scientist . . . explaining . . . parades of people drinking.

footage from Santo vs Dr Frankenstein and also Santo vs Capulina . . . modify it, flip it . . . disguise it, superimpose it. Actually do lots of superimposed intoxicos against stock backgrounds . . . that way we can just put him INTO other battles . . .

against kung fu guys, etc . . . imagine the hysterical mismatched fights . . . .

right, so just get him against blue . . . that blue card I have for a closeup. And I think I'll need an El Santo figurine for miniatures . . .

a clay santo for one segment . . . whatever, I do it quickly . . . animation . . . paper cut outs . . . Mix all my mediums into ONE BIG MESS . . . think of the soundtrack . . . think SPANISH . . . think cuban . . . recyle voices from family tapes . . . interesting voices . . . have two tapes "TALK" but not quite like on my radio play tapes . . . throw in sister miller as a matter of fact as an insane women commenting on the action every so often.

take the bearded surgeon from dr frankenstein vs santo . . . his closeups are priceless. he shows up a lot at a desk, so get him also conversing with this scientist . . . and then we can use this endless, boring science footage with lectures over it.

DR MURDER
EL INTOXICO . . .
is a mexican who knows the
full power of super kickpunch . . .
liquorfist kung fu! I respect . . .
HIS DREAMS AND IDEALS
of purest booze!
El Santo tries to sleep and assaulted by ninja at every turn. Eating breakfast, he's thawrted in the midst of getting his corn flakes. He throws the box at them, and hurts them in the kitchen. Intoxico continues drinking, then throws up on the ninja.

This monster has . . . the strength of ten men . . . but even ten men, is a lot less than the power . . . of the drunk man mexican!

And now . . . the legendary one 2-hour-sitting first draft of . . ."EL INTOXICO VS. NINJA", the proto Super-8 short that became a few segments of "CONTRA EL VICIO INFERNALE".

EL INTOXICO VS. NINJA
8/14/98 7:10 AM 666xlhyutyf5
fkfky99nbm.v-feex..ef34.fx-zc
The tender story of a mexican drunkard wrestler
and the ninja that loathed him
Cast of Values (1/2 off after 6PM):
El Intoxico. The hero, supposedly. Big, masked, mullet-haired and perpetually alcoholic. Bassy dubbed voice.

The Ninja. Arch enemy. Raving loon. Oily dubbed voice.

Captain Murray O' Groy. Peacekeeping irishman with a pipe and some vomiting problems. Hastily converted from the French Canadian.

Lt. Johnny Apeman. Good-natured Congo-masked assistant with an Amos n' Andy voice. Offensive, I suppose.

CAIFANO. Demented italian mob character actor. Plays the piano. Dies. Yells.

Gary J. Groy. Mysterious Gary Groy/Gary Busey/Nick Nolte cop character with a flask and a thick accent.

Lionel. Ninja middle management. Wanted to go into data entry, but his conscience told him to get into the ninja business.

Mexican One. Silent Santa Clausian mexican. Stares. Bad sex-change operation.

Mexican Two. Sings a sad, traditional mexican death song.

Mexican Three. Fondles traditional mexican furry worm.

Caifano's Thug One. Stabs pencils into hand. Soon learns to have wood impaled in his head.

Caifano's Thug Two. A good family man. Died tragically due to a botched tracheotomy.

Caifano's Thug Three. The most forgettable of the three thugs. Just kind of stood at the back.

Other Ninja. Ninja 1-29. A lot of Ninja that die frequently. Plenty of ninja = family entertainment. Book a ninja for your next bat mitzvah.

Mysterious Stranger. Whispers into O' Groy's ears. Dark unspeakable secrets that pad out the film.

Ext. Intro Barrage.

Credits roll throughout an intro sequence of ninja brutality. Unrelated examples of extreme violence. A few minutes of horribly cheap looking ninja impaling "normal folk" and throwing nails. You know, doing those ridiculously antisocial acts that only a ninja can do properly.

VOICEOVER:

The year was 1974. New Jersey was experiencing
one of the most devasting periods of ninja-caused
destruction since the late 19th century.
Using a combination of devious manipulation
coupled with strong recruitment methods,
ninja membership was at an all time high.
Aggressive drug sales techniques were used to
what some would call an excessive degree.

Have this over clips of Ninja abuse, ninja forcing strange powders into people faces, injections, the usual gore. Photos or maps of NJ. Also work in shots of the Ninja HQ, the bits with the chairman yelling into a CB radio. Have him bark orders into the CB, and of course hit himself with it repeatedly.

EXT. Crime Scene. Daylight or dusk.

The corpse of a previous ninja brutality is dribbling blood onto the floor. Tie, jacket,sunglass, and moustache-wearing guys poke around and put things in plastic bags. One "detective" wraps saran wrap around his face in a misguided effort to investigate. A camaro pulls up. Detective Gary J. Groy, the chainsmoking french canadian "guy" walks into frame. Smoking. Looking around. Suddenly he yells.

GARY J GROY:

There was fucking ninja here, man!

I can smell it!

This place fucking polluted by ninja!

DETECTIVE BOZO:

Well, Mr Groy…

GARY:

Call me Gary or GaryJ, you fucking tief!

BOZO:

Well, Gary…

it looks like the ninja struck again for

no apparent reason.

By my count, that's 17 dead.

130 this week. Grim figures, Gary.

GARY:

Fucking VC prick,

shut the hell up and let me think.

They must've been after something.

The ninja was doin' drug!

I

BOZO:

(not paying attention, continuing)

Well you see mr Gary, our stakeout here..

placed earlier on in the day on the suspicion that ninja

would be attracted to this landscape…

well, our stakeout . . . uh…
well, they're both dead.
GARY:
Dead from ninja?
You fuck!
BOZO:
Well, these ninja attacks are just really hurting the economy.
These ninja apparently have a point of contention
with the state of new jersey…
we have to find out why . . . why new jersey…
Bozo continues in this manner, droning monotonously. Groy
suddenly pipes up.
GARY:
I was in Nam you know,
I'm a fuckin veteran. NAM! NAM!
Remember NAM you prick!
I sweat in jungle! NAM!
Continues ranting about Nam while Bozo speaks. Finally he's
interupted by the phone ringing.
Int. Murray O' Groy's Office.
O'GROY:
Gary! Did you catch any ninja?
Heads are going to roll
if those ninja are still breaking laws.
EXT. Crime Scene. Daylight or dusk.
GROY:
No, I didn't get ninja.
Slippery cocksucker ninja kills all people and run…
They fly, jack.
Int. Murray O' Groy's Office.
O'GROY:
I don't care how fast they fly,
I want them eleminated,
Harold….
EXT. Crime Scene. Daylight or dusk.

GROY:

WHAT YOU MEAN?!!?

FUCKING HA-ROLD, jack?

Dis is fuckin Gary J. Groy, your brother…

fucking blood, man…

But you didn't fucking go to Nam…

Groy continues screaming into the phone until he hits Bozo with it for no reason. He follows this action up by tossing the phone away and suddenly screaming and going into a kung fu pose.

GROY:

KNIFE DISARM KUNG FU!!!!!!

BOZO:

Interior. O' Groy's Office.

JOHNNY:

Hemlow.

Dems here ninjasum be

causins da damagums.

Why, justum todaysum

da nin-ja be killins sebenteen men.

GROY:

This ninja is logistically out of control,

jack.

I want the entire department

working on ninja case…

All available men…

I'll bust that ninja's duff!

JOHNNY:

Hutum.

What I'ms be thinkins is dat we callsum

da man dey call El Intox-iCO!

O'GROY:

Is your brain working properly, Johnny?

You callin for themexican masked drunk-fight wrestler?

He knows the ways o fuckin stick-break gung-fu!

THAT STUFF IS DANGEROUS!

Improperly used,

it could result in death or at least serious injury.

JOHNNY:

Dasright…

He be kickins and punchsums da ninjasum.

He whats we need.

GROY:

I guess you right,

make call and get mexican in office!

Interior. El Intoxico's Apartment

Jump cut to establishing shot of a postcard of mexico, sensibly titled "Meanwhile in Mexico" Cut on over to a filthy hole. The key word is "filth". El Intoxico is lecturing to a small crowd (w/ straw hats) on his drunken wrestling techniques.

EL INTOXICO:

(smooth, deep voice dubbed from off-camera)

You see my friends,

the power of drunken fighting is a privilige

that mustn't be abused.

Channel the alcoholism and use it for justice.

And then use your ability for killing of bastard,

but only with a pure heart.

For that is the sacred code of the drunk-fighter.

Various squeals of encouragement from Intoxico's flunkies. The phone rings (or rather, an off-camera voice makes a telephone ring noise) and Intoxico knocks over a bunch of stuff while attempting to answer it.

EL INTOXICO:

(gasping, yelling into the phone)

HELLO! YES I AM HEARING YOU!

PLEASE TALK LOUDLY AND QUICKLY

FOR MAXIMUM COMPREHENSION!

WHAT'S THAT? YOU SAY….

You say that there is drug?

America, yes?

Well, I am in Mexico

and will be there within several days.

(slams down reciever, turns dramatically to camera and gestures)

I AM NOW GOING TO THE PLACE OF AMERICA!

TO FIGHT INJUSTICE AND BREAK THE HEADS

OF CRIMINILE ELEMENTS!

Loud sound effect and cut to——

Ext. Daylight. Various roads.

El Intoxico races through the countryside and down major highways at top speed whilst chugging alcohol. Running is intercut with maps. Clearly making good on his promise to arrive in America.

Fade out during triumphant music and Intoxico . . . yes, running.

INT. POLICE STATION COMPUTER ROOM.

Meet Ashish Sheth, police computer research/whatever guy. Ashish is of course getting porn/masturbating and kissing his hand seconds before O' Groy enters.

ASHISH:

Oh oh . . . super vga...

Ashish continues writhing when O'Groy enters.

O' GROY:

Ashish! What the flaming hell are you doing!

This is a professional police force with

credentials and a responsibility!

Not a pile of haggis!

ASHISH:

Dudeeeee, fuckin' research...

Uhhh . . . 640k ram!

O'GROY:

Straighten up and fly right!

Now, we need some help on this ninja case...

It's taxing all our resources and we need your skills.

ASHISH:

Dude. Like, try like-a search, man.

They got a website and advertise...

Some sort of sequence of ninja web pages detailing their plans.... Trumpet blasts, O'Groy yelling incoherently, zoom-ins to the eyes, etc.

O' GROY:

Ashish, why is this mouse sticky?

ASHISH:

Dude, don't bother me with details.

Dis is Ashish!

O'GROY:

That's it, I've seen enough.

We've got to stop this, it's . . . it's unspeakable.

Flagrant abuse of the law . . .

and I'm not going to stand for it.

We need El Intoxico's help!

Where is he?!?!

He should be here by now!

O'GROY marches out of the room.

ASHISH:

Jah, ok . . . .Jou're cool,

whatever . . . go to e-hella.....

Int. O'Groy's Office.

Groy is eating some sort of messy food, getting it all over himself. Johnny is pinning little flags to a big map of monmouth county to see if there's a pattern to these vile ninja attacks. Well, this scene was shot in spastic installments that would take an engineer to edit together properly.

GROY:

Whaddafuck?

It's been 3 days and ninja

out killin' like a fucking rodney!

Dis Intoxico is nothing but poppycock...

Pure fabrication...

JOHNNY:

Relaxums, mista Murray…

dis intoxico is beums commins from Mexicosum.

He be here's um soon.

GROY:

Well, I hope so…

before ninja kill all fucking baby and people.

Groy continues eating. El Intoxico barrels into the room spilling booze. Groy vomits for no apparent reason.

EL INTOXICO:

I came as soon as I heard about drug.

These ninja must pay the penalty-

and eat their sins back in pieces!

MURRAY:

Stop de ninja!

Do dis! Johnny!

Get me some pork chop.

Johnny scurries off to comply.

GROY:

(gesturing)

Dis map show all place where ninja attack.

It form a shape, der is a fuckin pattern, man.

Look here. Dese are pictures of ninja.

Pictures of bastard.

(obviously still photos over his narration)

EL INTOXICO:

I see and understand how grave

your situation is.

Ninja can be a cruel people that show no respect

for civilized society.

It is up to masked avengers like ourselves

to police the world and fight off the ninja.

For the glory of Mexico!

Intoxico gestures. Insert shot of mexicans chanting "FOR THE GLORY OF MEXICO!".

GROY:

If ninja take monmouth county,

mexico is next. We fuckin neighbors, jack.

Be on the lookout for hooded prick!

EL INTOXICO:

Right, my friend.

Do not fear or worry.

I will right the wrongs and punish

these men for their indiscretions.

No more will ninja plague new jersey!

Ext. Window. Daylight.

A ninja at the window observes the meeting and quickly phones
_____, the head evil ninja.

Int. Ninja HQ.

Shabby little HQ with goofy logo on the wall. 2 or 3 bored-looking ninja slouch around, possibly waving around lit torches for no discernable reason. The ferociously dull ninja chairman barks into a telephone.

CHAIRMAN:

Right. I see.

How foolish to send a mexican to do a man's job.

Right.

(hangs up phone)

Lionel! Get me caifano on the phone!

Ninja #7 peeks into doorway, yells, and runs off. The Chairman injects heroin. After some groaning, he picks up the phone.

Int. Caifano's Office.

Dimly lit "living room". Caifano sits idly typing into a laptop. Random doughy thug leans against a background wall with some crude weapon. Another random thug sits at the table, playing mumblypeg with a series of pencils. Throughout Caifano's conversation, he repeatedly stabs the pencil into his hand. And what a great scene this was. Caifano was marvelous as himself and really gave the scene some grandeur. Dan stabbed himself (and Caifano for some reason) repeatedly. Classic dining room cinema.

CAIFANO:

This is Caifano.

Talk to me you son of a bitch!

Int. Ninja HQ.

CHAIRMAN:

Ah yes, Caifano.

My favorate italian.

How are things in the prostitution business?

Int. Caifano's Office.

CAIFANO:

You never mind that.

Whaddahell do you want from me?

Int. Ninja HQ.

CHAIRMAN:

There's a certain masked mexican wrestler in town
that I want dealt with.

I want every bone broken and every ligament torn.

Please deliver his cartilage and large intestine
to my office by tommorow morning.

Int. interior. Caifano's Office.

CAIFANO:

Yeah. I'll take care of it. I gotta go type notes now.

Int. Ninja HQ.

CHAIRMAN:

Don't fail me, Caifano.

He's a devious mexican that might disrupt our drug trade.

Int. Caifano's Office.

Zoom out from telephone reciever. Caifano is frantically typing
notes on a cheap keyboard. He yells a bit.

CAIFANO:

Call the boys and send em out!

I wanna I wanna I wanna!

Horribly out-of-date WIPE on to:

Ext. daylight side of the road.

Intoxico is walking proudly down the street, perhaps saluting
passing civilians. Out of nowhere a pickup truck screeches to a

halt and an assortment of severely retarded men leap out waving pieces of wood around.

EL INTOXICO:

Cunning devils!

My wrestling ability will defeat you!

THUG:

Caifano doesn't like you!

Intoxico swigs from a bottle. Inept hand-to-hand combat is engaged. A hick gets a piece of wood impaled in his face. Much bloodshed. Much gesturing. Somehow they subdue him and drag around a dummy with the truck. He eventually overpowers and crucifies the thugs with potent gung-fu. Hmm, one throat-slicing effect . . . one wood impalement in the head.... Punch to the ground death. Vomiting. Blood pouring out of mouth. "Leaves in the face"

EL INTOXICO:

And so you die like the maggot that you are!

Justice is again maintained!

SCENE NINEBEEE Interior. Bar.

El Intoxico enters and sits down.

Drinking commences. Possible small talk with bartender and "patrons".

EL INTOXICO:

I tell you now,

fighting the criminal element causes you to come down with a powerful thirst for the alcohol.

I must then drown my stomach with the sauce.

El Intoxico yells various things at everyone. For no real reason a small fight breaks out and Intoxico allows himself some more kung fu extermination time. Perhaps a broken bottle gets stuck in a chest.

*****SCENE 10 interior. Caifano's office

Caifano is on the phone. Random thug clutches his bleeding hand.

CAIFANO:

What do you mean they're dead?

Fangul! Goddamn mexican!

Yeah. Yeah. Bye.

Caifano slams down the phone.

CAIFANO:

Goddamn wrestler!

Fucking japanese gonna kill me now!

Caifano clutches pistol and tenses up. The phone rings. Caifano fires. Random thug screams and slumps over.

CAIFANO

AHHHHHHHHH!

Caifano answers the phone.

CHAIRMAN: (v/o)

Caifano. You've failed me.

For this you must die.

Caifano drops reviever. Fires gun wildly.

CAIFANO:

AHHHHHHHHH!!!!!

Cheap knife is thrown into caifano's hand. Typical screaming.

Cut to a tv monitor playing a tape of the chairman laughing hysterically shouting.

CHAIRMAN:

GOOD. GOOD.

VERY GOOD.

******SCENE ELEVEN. Interior. Groy's office.

Groy reads memo on clipboard and laughs.

GROY

I was no friend of Cai-fan-oo,

but this ninja business gotta stop, jack!

I know what this is, drug is involved.

I was in army, I know what drug is.

JOHNNY:

Dis be's ans important case.

I gonna be thinkins that I sho should go downs to the ninja and bust dose caps on dems headsums.

Right on.

Johnny picks up weapon of some kind.

GROY:

You be careful, wait for El Intoxico.

Fuckin ninja don't fire blanks. Eclis.

JOHNNY:

I'msgots ta does my part.

For the glory of the poleece.

For my mammy and pappy, yessir...

I goin ta shows duh ninjas whats death is.

GROY:

Well, be fuckin careful is what Groy say.

JOHNNY:

Yassir.

And I'ms gonna come back

and brings ya ninja blood sausage.

GROY:

I hope so, Johhny.

Because you know how much I love budan.

********SCENE TWELVE Interior. Ninja HQ.

CHAIRMAN:

God damn, the ninja are doing good...

good.. very good.

Our competition is eliminated

and the heroin flows freely into all the elementary schools.

Our forced addiction program is going quite well.

(V/O over footage of ninja shoving powder down people's orifi from the next scene) AHAHAHAHAHAHHAHA!

(abrubt stop)

RIGHT!

8SCENE THIRTEEN. Outdoors. Anywhere. Daylight.

El Intoxico, walking down the street just happens to pass a mean ninja carelessly forcing drugs on some "guy".

EL INTOXICO:

You hooligans!

By the power of alcohol I command you to stop molesting that citizen!

NINJA:

Fuck off, El Intoxico

I need to make a living.

EL INTOXICO:

Inhospitable bastard!

Don't make me . . . hurt you!

NINJA:

I'd like to see...

you try and hurt me!

EL INTOXICO:

Right.

Now I'm going to kill you.

Abrubt standing jump kick directly into ninja. Either trampoline or badly stop motion animated. Ninja screams and spits out much blood. Intoxico approachs the ninja's corpse and tears off the hood. TRUMPET BLAST! It's a hideous zombie!

SWISH CUT TO

Int. Ninja HQ.

CHAIRMAN:

Good, good. Very good.

The ninja zombification methods have provided us

with an army of atomic zombies,

driven only by a lust for a blood. Very good!

There will be no stopping my vile minions of the mangoat!

HAH-HAHhohaho. HAH-HAHhohaho. HAH-HAHhohaho!

NINJA:

Boss, I don't trust these zombies.

CHAIRMAN:

Oh, but you must.

Because they are going to allow our total domination of new jersey!

My army of contempt will rape the land...

VERY GOOD!

NINJA:

Boss, these zombies might turn on us.

CHAIRMAN:

You decrepit campy bastard!

The atomic zombie supermen obey me!

I'm the master! I point the way!

HA HA HA HA HA!

GET READY FOR TOTAL ATOMIC NINJA ANNIHILATION!

Ah-HA ah ah ha ha haw!

EXT. Roads or Hoboken.

Johnny Apeman races through the streets or suburbs in a spastic manner, accompanied by ridiculously inappropriate music.

Int. Ninja HQ.

LIONEL:

(mincing assistant ninja speaks up, maybe staring into a monitor. Cutaway to footage of Apeman running)

Boss,

what looks like an ape is approaching.

He looks like trouble.

CHAIRMAN:

Right.

Go on and send out some of the zombie-

ninja to take car of this little ape.

Zoom in to his eyes. Dramatic chord. Awkward pause.

CHAIRMAN:

(nintendo kung fu laugh over and over again)

AH-HA—HA . . . HA . . . HA!

Ext. Ninja HQ building.

Two ninja stand outside with torches lit. Johnny Apeman walks up.

NINJA #1:

We said nobody can come so nobody's going to come.

NINJA #2:

They never said somebody

was going to come so nobody's going to come.

NINJA #1:

Somebody's going to come but no

because nobody is going to come.

NINJA #2:

Right, we can't allow anyone to come.

Nobody is allowed to come.

NINJA #1:

No police here.

Apeman suddenly lunges and defuses the two ninja with moderate gung fu. Johnny cuts them up to make blood sausage. Apeman brushes himself off and enters the building.

Int. Bar.

El Intoxico continues to drink. Murray O' Groy enters. O' Groy drinks.

O' GROY:

El Intoxico!

What are you doing here?

EL INTOXICO:

Honing my drunken-fighting skills

by continuous practice.

O' GROY:

That's all well and good,

but Johnny went to fight those damn ninja…

BY HIMSELF!

EL INTOXICO:

My friend, He'll be torn apart!

His kung fu isn't anywhere near good enough!

It's weak!

O'GROY:

You've got to help him.

EL INTOXICO:

RIGHT!

O'GROY:

You've GOT to help him!

Because you see . . . he's not only my partner...
But . . . El Intoxico, he's my . . . my lover.
EL INTOXICO:
I understand the love you share.
O'GROY:
O'GROY:
Just in case,
I gave my brother Gary J O'Groy a call.
His kung fu is very good indeed.
(Intoxico goes on a long long long rant about nothing in particular while O'Groy purchases booze from the bartender and gives it to that charming masked wrestler.)
O'GROY:
You're going to need this to boost your strength, mlad.
Only permanent liver damage can save you now!
EL INTOXICO:
In this reasoning you are correct.
Now, I must be off to the devious ninja headquarters
to pound the fear of Yahweh into them.
O' Groy:
Remember to bring back some blood sausage for my family.
EL INTOXICO:
(while racing off)
RIGHT!
Ext. daylight road
More bits of Intoxico-running-down-the-street-drinking footage. A ninja on a roof watches him.
EL INTOXICO:
(calm v/o)
I had to reach the ninja filth-hole soon,
if I intended to save Johnny from a slow, painful death.
Did he deserve to die?
Was there some crime in him?
Have I drank enough?
El Intoxico kneels down to pray.

EL INTOXICO:
I beseech thee and worship all gods of liquor.
Alcoholic spirits, hear my call.
Let me gain the courage of drinking
and the knowledge of brutal alcoholism.
For mexico's glory and until the armageddon!
ALCOHOL!
A superimposed very silly "old god" face is superimposed over his plea.
DEUS EX ALCOHOLICA:
(booming, heavily reverbed voice)
ELLLLLLL INTOXICOOOOOOOOOOO!
EL INTOXICO:
I feel myself replenshed with the energy
of generations of drunkards.
My wrestling skills are at their peak
and I feel I'm ready to take on Pitch himself.
Yah!
Intoxico swills more liquor. The Ninja fires a rifle from the roof and attacks.
Much violence and yelling ensues. Pow bash biff hurt yell. They scream the name of their techniques before attacking, as per the usual kung fuhell. The ninja runs away.
EL INTOXICO:
RICKMAN! RICMAAANNN!
I Know it was you!
San Felipe, 1984.
I never forget a face!
RICKKKMAAAAN!
INT. NINJA HQ.
CHAIRMAN:
Stupid idiot!
Defeated by that masked man!
NINJA:
But, Boss. He's a good wrestler.

CHAIRMAN:

I don't care if he's Leaping Lanny Popoff!

If you fail me again,

I'll kill you and make you a zombie!

You'll be dead like the rest!

NINJA:

Sorry, Boss.

It must be my reactive mind.

CHAIRMAN:

Your reactive mind is going to get you into a lot of trouble someday...

Xenu isn't going to appreciate it...

NINJA:

I don't want to offend you, boss...

But.. You're crazy!

CHAIRMAN:

That might be the case...

But my insanity is perfect, like a diamond.

Like a very good diamond . . . very good....

Int. Ninja HQ.

LIONEL:

Boss, our men are dead.

And El Intoxico is here to visit.

CHAIRMAN:

No problem.

Send out some ninja

while I sacrifice someone to Satan

to gain demonic wrestling power!

At this point it goes into a Sho Kosugi elaborate "suiting-up, doing bad tai-chi" nonsense set to overblown soundtrack music.

Ext. Daylight.. Ninja HQ Building.

Intoxico arrives on the scene and quickly examines the unconscious ninja. He kicks one for entertainment . The body moans and vomits blood.

EL INTOXICO:

Disgusting bastard!

GARY J GROY:

(appears out of nowhere waving pistol around)

Hold the fuck up, jack.

EL INTOXICO:

(turns around, gestures yet again)

Who in the nine hells are you?

GARY:

Eclis, man.

Dis is Gary . Groy...

I' m with poe-lice.

EL INTOXICO:

Is that so?

I'm mightily impressed.

GARY:

I better fuckin' go wit you to kill

Eagle Lake Ninja before Fort Kent is surrounded.

EL INTOXICO:

Well. My friend. Right.

Yes! Well, be you careful is what I suggest.

Thank you, then.

Ext. Outside Ninja HQ.

Groy and Intoxico cautiously look. 2 Ninja jump in out of nowhere and do bad kung fu. Someone, possibly Groy . . . vomits. Fighting. Etc. Etc.

GARY J. GROY:

Vietnam taught me wall, jack.

Knife-disarm kung fu work like a charm...

EL INTOXICO:

I understand,

but I must tell you that alcohol increases

fighting comprehension.

GROY:

Waitaminute, man. Dis fucking Ninja is something else...

I know what this is...
Groy rips off ninja hood to reveal a bad zombie effect.
GROY:
Dis is zombie!
EL INTOXICO:
Yes of course I know this, my friend.
I just didn't want to get you alarmed...
Now, we need to figure out a way in...
Int. Ninja HQ.
LIONEL:
That goddamn whore-bastard.
Boss, his kung fu is good.
We didn't count on that.
CHAIRMAN:
Well of course his kung fu is good-
he's mexican! What did you expect?
LIONEL:
Boss, I think we should run away right now.
Right?
CHAIRMAN:
You cowardly BASTARD!
The ninja never run.
LIONEL:
Boss, I think that strategically speaking,
it's our best option.
CHAIRMAN:
(watching El Intoxico fighting footage on a small monitor)
Well, I suppose you're right.
Get the jet ready.
LIONEL:
Right boss.
Just come this way.
Int. Miniature Hell
GI Joe plane "flying".
CHAIRMAN(vo)

I doubt there's a mexican alive
that can stop a jetplane in midair.
That bastard is going to pay for all this...
The ninja attempt to escape in the plane. Cut to cheesy jet interior. El Intoxico races outside the building and throws a rope on the jet, pulling it back to earth. The ninja eject without parachutes and just leap down.
SCENE TWENTY-TWO: FINAL FIGHT HOLOCAUST MORTAL BODY BLOW HOLDS BARRED
Trampolines used excessively. Fighting fighting and more fighting While Intoxico handles Lionel, a ninja seemingly Groy.
REVENGE FOR YOU
SCENE TWENTY-THETHREE
Interior. Shitty, filthy bedroom.
Intoxico is sprawled on the bed smoking the foul weed with roots in hell and eating hot pockets (maybe show him microwaving them in the kitchen as well). He's watching Dolemite or any Rudy Ray film. Suddenly Gary Groy bursts in.
GARY GROY:
Intoxico!
What the fuck you doing smoking drug
and eating da hotpocket?
You fucking lazy bastard...
EL INTOXICO:
My friend,
I need some time to recuperate
between wrestling matches.
GARY:
Get fuckin going, jack!
Ninja are out there!
Everywhere!
Be careful around fucking Ninja,
they smart!
EL INTOXICO:
Just give me a minute to get going and prepare.

Intoxico "does" a nitrous cannister whilst Gary J. Groy yells in the background.

GARY:

Hurry up, you prick-bastard!

They in a car driving fast like bastard!

INTOXICO:

The drug's hold is great...

I need to gain strength.

Intoxico drinks heavily. Gestures.

INTOXICO:

And now at last I have the power

of burning hot booze within me.

The alcohol flows through my bloodstream!

Intoxico races out of the room.

GARY:

Mexicans are fuckin crazy, jack.

After a car chase, the ninja "leader" while running ponders whether or not he should sacrifice someone to satan for help. He does. The infernal wrestling match kills intoxico, turning him into an undead wrestler who needs to eat human flesh to stay alive. He chases after the ninja. Final battle. The ninja reveals himself to be Groy. Much death ensues. ! Bluescreened final battle-silly anime "hyperspace" lines chromakeyed in. Explosion footage Horrible injury is the final result .

Intoxico burns himself alive. Citizens ponder the meaning of existence and the drunken wrestler up in the sky watching us all. His image is dissolved in slowly. Mexican music swells. Roll credits and outtakes.

CHAPTER EPSILON.

PRODUCTION MEMO FOUND IN GARBAGE AND GLUED BACK TOGETHER

(EXCERPTS)

First up......

_____SCENE THE FOURTH exterior. Daylight. Various roads.

_____SCENE SIXTEEN exterior daylight road

El Intoxico running down the street n' drinking shots

AND THEN:

_____SCENE ONE

Intro credit sequence barrage

_____SCENE SIX exterior. Window. Daylight.

Brief shot of ninja peaking into window and making a phone call.

_____SCENE NINE exterior daylight side of the road.

Big fight scene. El Intoxico vs 3 retarded men. Car pulling dummy (this can be filmed later next week, once we make a dummy)

Break. And later on....

_____SCENE SEVEN interior. Ninja HQ.

_____-SCENE THIRTEEN Interior. Ninja HQ.

_____SCENE EIGHTEEN Interior. Ninja HQ.

Various Ninja Chairman on the phone, talking to assistant ninja, etc. Kosugi-ripoff tai-chi scene.

another wrestler . . . bluesilver mask, blue shirt, white pants.

Santo/Intoxico: rapeman mask, tan turtleneck, brown or black slacks. Then we can use the footage from Dr. Frankenstein.

Cut out animation or poor cel animation intro credits sequence with a stirring Mexican theme.

Walking . . . lots of talking . . . pad things out with small room discussions . . . fighting..runing walking

Capulina . . . warehouse fight scene. Santo with a jacket and a t-shirt under it . . . white . . . black pants . . . fighting several thugs in front of cardboard . . . . intercut with this stuff. Cardboard boxes falling on people.

guy thowing knives at Intoxico.

establishing shot of caifano's place

CHAPTER GAMMA. Secret Sweet Valley High Diaries Excerpts. 6/17/97 11:18 PM

Apparently I'm in the midst if writing the script you just read. The rest of the film came in today. I've got a huge pile of film boxes sitting here. Mocking me. Well, looks like it's time to begin. Break the Belly statis by spitting out something quickly and filming it veryveryverysoonafter.

20 k40 sound 50 min

11 k40 silent 27.5

4 plusx 10

6 ektachrome 15

Order more next week. 10 ekta, 10 more k40 sound. Still, it's plenty to do this intoxico film and then begin Belly. Unproduced screenplays: Family of Filth, Space Vampires from Dimension Zero, and something else the name of which is a vague memory. Hopefully these will be destroyed.

A powerful reminder of unfullfilled actions-

6/19/97 2:15:25 AM

Yow. Filmed several scenes from El Intoxico vs Ninja today. Caifano was a riot as CAIFANO . . . I'm so glad my father finally broke down and "acted". He was pretty damn funny. Groy gave a bunch of excuses to stay at home so Joe stepped in as a more Irish O'Groy. So inept it was perfect. We also did a mexico scene in the basement.... All in all, 4 rolls shot. So tommorow I'd like to do a bunch of exteriors and one fight scene.

6/19/97 3:10:44 PM

Well, I wonder if we're going to film much today.

6/23/97 3:23:48 AM

We'll be shooting more "El Intoxico" footage wed. and Thursday . . . Hopefully we can finish it off by Saturday . . . Where some nyc wandering needs to take place . . . (Mes gots ta drops off'das brack and whitums veeeversal filmsum.) And maybe I'll finally develop those 3 rolls of ancient 16mm.

Which I think was animation, ninja drug holocaust in my grandmother's apartment, and philly garbage.

6/24/97 1:06:59 AM

Monkey Kung Fu. There's quality filmmaking.

(retarded, horribly secret specialized kung fu techniques with long indecipherable names)

Blazing Locust Blood-Pig Style
Horrible Bloated Wound Goat Monkey technique
Seven Golden Dung Beetle Air Conditioner Dragon Fist Style
Kung Fu
Monstrous Antellope Grease Kung Fu
Feeble-Minded Big Power Kick of Vicious Hurt
Scar-minded Blood Head Murder Style Kung Fu
Son of a Bitch Style Chin-Wound Fight-Style Kung Fu
Brown Vest Monkey Fist Explosion Fu
Deadly Snake Moustache Hate Tiger Kung Fu
Power Leap of a Parasite Violent Style
Powerful Mutilation Snake Desecration Secret kung fu
Bowl Headed Blood Bastard Molecular Kung FU
Throbbing Vomit Punch Kung Fu
6/26/97 12:18:20 AM
Farmingdale Gospel Hour
Cancer Ward Children being tormented as the basis of a game
show.

Anyway, tommorow we continue filming El Intoxico. Probably
a mix of exterior nonsense and the Ninja HQ interiors.

Belly full of anger: larry wu with taped-up "anonymous" mask?
Pale blue with a "good" "oriental" shirt of some type? It could
probably work. How about Umberto? A non-mask wearer would
probably be a good idea. Some ethnicy type with a pencil-thin
moustache. Ack! Athlete mask with a "character moustache".

Belly is going to have to be profoundly cheap-looking. Mask-
wearing characters that don't attract attention seem to be a viable
gimmmmick. Then we could shoot it fast n' slightly less painfully.

More bluescreen and animation-
6/28/97 1:25:39 AM
No filming today. Suppose I'll go to new york tommorow to
develop film and spend money.

Twitching research develops a clear plan and modern gains-
based system for traffic redirection in the year 1870 . . . Falling
drunks explain patiently that the best route to point pleasant is

attached to his cranial sockets. Failing this, gasoline is spread throughout the valley and slowly lapped up by converted hermaphrodite realtors.

7/4/97 2:49 AM

The computer is all different shades of fucked up and has been for weeks. Everything is configured improperly and it's giving me a headache. Gee, can't wait for the fun of trying to get the editing system up and running.

3 Intoxico rolls came back today. They look "nice", everything is just about ok except for 2 out of focus shots. And it's at 18fps. ARGHHHHHHHHHHHHHHHHHHHHHHHHHHHHHHHHHH.

Besides that, the color is creamy and the lighting is suprisingly acceptable. Joe's "acting" as Murray O' Groy is actually pretty hysterical.

I wonder how long I can remain employed at "Janet Studio". What a hideous joke that place is . . . horrible shrieking bitchy Janet and the meddling cancer-ridden husband writing silly memos to himself. The usual torment that goes hand in hand with employement is an ever-present tangible . . . Ugh. At least the money is good. The computer is finally paid off.

7/5/97 6:03 PM

Idea-Puppetzar 5 . . . A horribly cheap puppetmaster ripoff with extremely silly dolls(sock puppet, Ben Franklin, Claymation nonsense, Crow, etc). An old demented Toulonesque character lets his killer puppets run around and cause havoc)

So X-day has begun. Shot 3 rolls of El Intoxico outdoor footage today.... The running scene and a short battle with an extremely silly ninja. Tommorow we'll be shooting some MORE running footage, another outdoor ninja barbecue, and the bar scenes with Murray O'Groy.

FGH:

Credits in the middle of the show . . . Start off as a different show ALWAYS, and then go into a silly super8 and video intro. El Intoxico will be used for the show and shown in chunks with the same intro and a "previously on El Intoxico" bit. And we can pad out 5-10 minutes per show with the usual "live music" and collagefilm heresies.

7/7/97 1:19 AM

Filmed the Intoxico bar scene today in Joe's basement. Murray O'Groy confessed his love for johnny apeman. A silly fight broke out. Santa yelled a bit. 4 rolls all in all. I hope they weren't out of focus, that camera is acting very screwy. I'll have to buy a new one soon...

Intoxico: against a black background film stock shots of El Intoxico yelling, posturing, kung fu gestures, and CU punches and kicks. Insert them into the other fight scenes.

VOICEOVER:

The year was 1974. New Jersey was experiencing one of the most devasting periods of ninja-caused destruction since the late 19th century. Using a combination of devious manipulation coupled with strong recruitment methods, ninja membership was at an all time high. Aggressive drug sales techniques were used to what some would call an excessive degree. It was up to THIS MAN, captain Murray O' Groy . . . to put a stop to this reign of hooded terror. But, he couldn't handle the job . . . so cheap foreign labor was employed.

Have this over clips of Ninja abuse, ninja forcing strange powders into people faces, injections, the usual gore. Photos or maps of NJ.

Add another 3 scenes to the middle/buhginnin, and pad the ending out for like 8-10 minutes. Stupid car chase scene to another location. Intoxico running at full speed after the car.

Intoxico drinking too much during a battle. Much throwing up. So he fails. Gary Groy dies, or appears to. Silly screaming "REVENGE FOR YOU"

MORE intro scenes of ninja attacks on the population. Have O'Groy try to deal with the problem himself . . ."investigating" the "crime scene" . . . ah! So they call in Larry Wu to do the scene with the coffee spilling...

Printer, modem and sound working. Tommorow I'll get the CDR fired up and finish contractual obligations.

To get more footage for extra dialogue, transfer zoomed in to a cu/ecu, backwards, different speeds, etc. Of course, you could also loop it in premiere. From now on, shoot a little film of the sets without any actors, for possible bluescreen use if some footage is blurry. That way we could do it in video and chromakey the super8 set footage.

Hmm, the scott footagee can be him telling O'groy the fact that the ape is dead. Cut to silly "dream" sequence of O' Groy screaming "Johnny", them running in a field arm in arm, etc. Cut back to O'groy sobbing hysterically. He then kills himself either by rifle or wrist-slitting. Or both. He could fail at shooting himself...

The ninja manage to inject El Intoxico with nameless "Drug". He goes on a wild hallucinatory rampage, claymation horrors everywhere, masks, etc etc. He finally manages to counter the effects through the power of drinking.

This might expand into feature length, the rate which new scenes are being added. Maybe we can pad it out using almost all footage and recycling some for extra dialogue . . . to about 70 minutes. I think I'll give Groy the script . . . see if he could write a few me scenes and fuck up the dialogue a bit.

Written, produced, animated, and directed by

Ontor Pertawst

Executive Producer

Gary Ignotofsky

Director of Photography

Johnny Amoco

Sound

Rodney Realistic

El Intoxico Stunt Doubles

Alan Linnet

Santa Claus Audioanimatronics by

Dan Smith

arring

Ian Smith

As El Intoxico
And Bar Drunk Two
Joe Linett
As Murray O' Groy
And Bartender
And Mexican Three
Chris Roy
As Gary J. Groy
And Ninja CEO
Dan Smith
As Johnny Apeman
And Bar Drunk One
And Ninja
And Caifano's Personal Assistant
And Mexican One
Caifano
As Caifano
Amber Degrutolla
As Mexican Two
Scott K.
As The Mysterious Stranger
7/7/97 9:37 PM

Spent the day fussing with Premiere to make simple animations . . . using premiere's "bitching "keying/trasparencies stuff. I
likes its. I'm really going to be able to do a lot of the inevitable
"stuff" once the editing equipment is snagged. Suppose I'll be
hooking it all up next week.

7/8/97 8:42 PM

Got back some RL rolls (Andy Hitler, Werewolf Total Recall,
etc. etc. etc.) today. And a bit from Intoxico. Caifano is hilarious.
The RL rolls are a bit . . . uh, something. As usual. I'm working
on the El Intoxico poster . . . should be finished tonight…

I never felt a head start in which death concludes the acts of
screenwriting. Please consider this the next time you lose track of
what happens to Lee. Other performance addresses are kept on file

to maintain the integrity of freeze-frames locked inside cabinets. And fine cabinets, too. Really yellow.

Looks like I have enough to shoot everything in the current script all the way up to scene 21.For the final "conflict" and any of the extra padding, I'm going to have to buy more. Maybe I should order another 40 rolls.

Get my grandmother to narrate a section of it . . . or better yet, the intros to all the scenes with el intoxico in them.

7/10/97 12:09 AM

Groy-assisted idea meltdown subrainsturmandrang

Ninja sends a woman (he hypnotizes her with christmas lights on his mask) to seduce el intoxico, she gives him a hallucinogenic brew. Goes on rampage. Kills.

Ninja sacrifices a girl to satan to help him defeat el intoxico. A demon wrestler appears. Fights Intoxico in an infernal wrestling ring.

Eye gouging.

Ninja removes his mask and he's Gary Groy.

Crime scene intro. Groy AND Groy investigating. I know what this is . . . this is drug. Ninja drug."

"The chief is leaving"

Intoxico drinks and breaths fire.

El intoxico is a masochist. Women whip him.

He becomes a pothead in the middle of the movie, sits around watching shitty movies while eating hot pockets. Then a groy pours booze down his throat so he snaps out of it.

Dual unmasking during the final fight.

BACK TO NORMAL.

Gosh, what productivity. Shot 7 rolls of Intoxico footage: the ninja headquarters stuff (fuck up the colors somehow on this stuff. . . maybe filters), the outdoor ninja-forcing-drugs-on-some-guy that turns into another Intoxico brawl, more running footage, an improptu brawl near "Happy Family" featuring the "c'mon you, c'mon you" guy, etc. So we're getting there. Tommorow I'm think-ing we should do more exteriors-in a park, maybe some of the hallucination stuff, the ninjabrutality stuff from the intro . . . Maybe the "somebodiesgonnacome,nobodie'sgonnacome" apeman scene...

TO DO:

Next:

Scene two and eleven: (reshoot o'groy/apeman bits)

Scene 9: big outdoor fight scene. Dragging dummy around.

Scene 19: inside ninja hq, in some large room. Typical ninja vs. intoxico fight scenes

Scene 21: goofy gi joe jet "miniature. Rope pulling jet

Scene 22: intoxico pulling plane down with rope. Brief fighting.

Scene 23: car chase. Cheap.

Tobewritten:

Ninja hypnotizing woman with christmas tree lights

Woman seducing Intoxico

Bedroom: partial nudity, Intoxico takes drugs.

Intoxico Freakout deathrampage hallucinogenic hell

Ninja considering a sacrifice to help in his intoxico crusade

Ninja satanic sacrifice. Satan appears.

El Intoxico is sent to hell by bad special effects

Intoxico vs Stupid Demon in an infernal wrestling match.

O'Groy in his office sobbing and reminescing about johnny. He kills himself.

Intoxico becomes a pothead and sits around. O'Groy gets him going.

Gary Groy killing someoen with a star or throwing knife, for no real reason.

Finished:

Scene 7: ninja hq, calling caifano

Scene 12: ninja hq, chairman and lionel

Scene 18: ninja hq, chairman doing stupid kosugi "getting ready" scene

Scene 20: ninja hq, lionel and chairman talking

Scene 13: outdoor. Ninja addicting citizen with drugs. Intoxico intervenes.

Shoot another 3 rolls for Dan's Mistake: color outdoor/CGI hallucinations, and then a stern moral by a suited guy at the end. Hmm, come to think of it . . . as an intro as well.

Wait-the post crime scene . . . just Gary Groy investigating . . . he calls Murray O' Groy.

Have a corpse, and a guy in a jacket and tie around.

Crime Scene. Daylight or dusk.

The corpse of a previous ninja brutality is dribbling blood onto the floor. Tie, jacket,sunglass, and moustache-wearing guys poke around and put things in plastic bags. One "detective" wraps saran wrap around his face in a misguided effort to investigate. A camaro pulls up. Detective Gary J. Groy, the chainsmoking french canadian "guy" walks into frame. Smoking. Looking around. Suddenly he yells.

7/10/97 10:54 PM

Acted like a bastard at work. They didn't pay what they owed me for like 2 weeks. ARGH. Richard Kiel is on tv right now. Acting.

Tommorow:

Scene six: ninja peeking in window, making a phone call

Scene one (ninja brutality, possibly with more forced drug abuse, bystanders giving ninja opinions)

Scene1b: Crime Scene. Gary J Groy.

Scene 14: outside ninja hq. 2 ninja vs. apeman fight

Scene 17: outside ninja hq, intoxico kicks ninja corpse

7/12/97 6:03 PM

Accomplished zero filming this weekend. My.

7/13/98 6:34 AM

Ninja is also a pathetic "mad scientist", creating zombies or somesuch.

7/22/98 3:34 AM

Spent today continuing to agonize over "the budget". Edited the Murray O Groy scenes in premiere, currently testing out different filters. If I can grab cinelook, I think I might just pad out intoxico with DV footage completely screwed up . . . But tommorow I'm going to order yet another 500-600 worth of Super-

8 film . . . I definetely should be stockpiling the stuff in case I go through another period with no money (arghhhhhmustgetwork).

Later today It's time to shoot more Intoxico footage. At the least a ninja attack, the Groy crime scene, and the waste product sequence. Should've done this two weeks ago. Now that I'm not working, I should try to do some Intoxication filming every day.

More gore effects–try to come up with some digital intoxico "efx" as well-Intersperse bluescreened shots of Intoxico through lots of fight scenes. Shoot a bunch of different stances, poses, gestures, etc etc . . . Always remember to grab some empty landscape footage to have underneath . . . There's also that roll of car-window footage. Played at high speed that might be interesting.

Whatever is rendering now I'm just going to toss out. Maybe just save the sound-track . . . projector/camera "transfers" would come out much nicer in DV (also a good backup)...

Never thought to turn the monitor around and type in bed. Such burning hot comfort.

Just played around with the stop motion capabilities. Interesting. High quality animation with just a few thousand enter key pressings. I should definetly start churning out short animations again for FGH.... An intro sequence comes first.. And then the Claymation bits for Intoxico . . . his hallucination sequence.... Hmm, maybe also stop-motion some of the gestures and poses . . . then I can bring frames into photoshop and filterize specific parts . . . glows would work nicely, for fists or just his entire body...

Speaking of filters, cinelook sounds delicious. If I can somehow grab a pirated version, this might just be the ticket to give the Belly-shot DV footage some cheesy 8-16mm style . . . and occasional bursts of the film damage filter would work too, some scratches, hair, splices, stuttering, etc, now and then would be pretty slick. I imagine the rendering would take forever. Let's see

.... 7 seconds a frame . . . God, weeks of rendering, probably. This would definetly be something to apply to individual scene AVIs overnight..

Found Premiere 5. Now to snag the After Effects "family" of

"products". I'm glad I never really have to pay for software . . . those adobe bits are ridiculously expensive. Such value!

7/25/98 7:16 PM

Horrible horrible tragedy. Since the viewfinder was broken, ALL the rest of the intoxico footage is completely wasted. God. I can't believe it, and I haven't quite figured out what to do next.

7/26/98 5:37 AM

Pretty much another wasted day.

Reorganized the gear and such. It's a bit easier to work on in this arrangement.

You know, Intoxico was never meant to be a feature anyway. It's best to just shoot a few rolls to finish it off and then bury it. I'm sure once I get the equipment all these "plans" will change. I really should have tried to get this gear earlier, I mean I really needed the ability to shoot as much as I want to and instantly view the results . . . And just as instantly digitize and edit . . . Nonlinear editing opens up so many possibilities, so many ways of organizing and assembling different layers of video and sound . . . that although rendering time is slow . . . the benefits make it worth it.. especially now that I have so much expensive effects software (still no cinelook, which I hope will work out real well . . . the tests I've done with the crippled demo show a lot of potential, even though I haven't gotten film damage to work yet . . . and that's just as important as the grain simulation . . . I really would like the ability to add dirt and scratches....) It's pathetic the way I got so film snobbish, probably due to NYU, sure the look can't be beat . . . but it's friggin' expensive! (sidenote: this firesign live b&w video is great, I really should try to contact elayne and thank her for all these tapes...) I mean, 16mm looks great, and super8 is a fun format, but it's just plain stupid to stick with them exclusively . . . when video can be used to develop ideas inexpensively. Now that this DV stuff is available, higher quality stuff can be shot . . . and generation loss is minimized . . . plus the ability to use the existing computer to edit and use high-end effects is an irresistable draw.

7/31/98 7:58 AM

Everything is running smoothly now. Reread that Ed Wood book cover to cover. Picked up an Al Adamson book . . . apparently spun off of that psychotronic interview I read years ago...

I really should get a move on with El Intoxico. I was supposed to have it finished by the end of August . . . that's one month, plenty of time to finish shooting. Failing that, I think I should get a hold of "Devil Girls" and adapt it.

8/1/98 10:57 AM

Corpse Grinders is a fine film.

Watching "Racket Girls" right now. Timothy Farrell is a god among men. More lame wrestling in the movie! Sunday we should film the outdoor fight scenes, possibly Intoxico's drunken training with just Chris.

8/2/98 4:31 AM

Watched Faster Pussycat and Supervixens . . . Today we're going to shoot some outdoor scenes for El Intoxico . . . and probably some Groy scenes as well. It helps to watch movies constantly while filming. I think I'm finally over the tragic lost of a chunk of film, I think we can still pull this off as a feature . . . MIGHT AS WELL!

So I have to reshoot. Let's see-the cheap ninja guys all wear the blue "oriental mask" . . . this will make it more acceptable when we have the same guy die a few times.

I'm about to transfer a bunch of RL footage. Might as well start putting episode 201 together.

So Cinelook is alright I suppose-though high quality video is needed for it unless you want the stepped-on 8mm effect. I better get a move on and actually send out the fucking check for that gear. Aww, fuck it. Intoxico will be an incoherent mess of Super-8 and DV footage. Deadline: end of august. Until then, insane filmmaking and miles of footage shot. Then in Sept I get another editing job, edit the hell out of Intoxico and turn it into a 70-80 minute feature as intended with crazy music and a cd spinoff. While I edit it, we start filming Belly Full of Anger the same way . . . demented and mask-sporting nonsense quickly edited with noise music. Might as well make them surreal little movies to make up for the total lack of money. Then, we try to get working on Devil Girls or some sort of Russ Meyer/Ed Wood combined "hommage" DV feature with strippers and ridiculous dialogue. Crank the two through cinelook, with tedious filtering of individual segments and occasional damage. Full plate. I want all three to be shot and edited by next spring, and possibly a fourth in the works.

Spent so far:

Buz	200
Hard drive and memory	450
Cash for film and etc	200
Kodak charge	200
Camera package	2200
amazon	100
reel	80
internet	100
3530	
1210	
something weird	90

I think Belly Full of Anger is going to wind up being heavily bluescreened. I think the whole look

Of it would be more interesting with lots of FX, glows, stop-motion animation, keyed-in sets to give it a stylized, faked look . . . an internal stiffness in the film to match the dubbing. Christ, definetly DV plus cinelook. What was I thinking with this super-8 junk. If I mailed the check I would have had the camera by now to shoot today's scenes . . . and I think cinelook could do a decent job attempting to join all this footage together . . . Intoxico will be a test-run for the more intense, much more edited final product.

Belly Full of Anger will be letterboxed. Mask out the monitor slightly while shooting and always use the wideangle lens unless a zoom-to-the-eyes is needed. For Belly, I need to refine my directing "technique" and learn to get it done faster. Probably I think I need to do a master shot or two, and then a barrage of different angles to edit in, not having sound really helps here.. or having partial sync sound . . . but the main characters should be dubbed since the masks will make them unintelligable.

Down the line I'm going to get a RAID and a decent DV card. As of now, this will work and last a good 6 months or so, enough to do a few features on . . . and if they don't sell, who cares. At least down the line I'll have a "back catalog" to plunder. I also think I should get into more use of stock footage to pad things out and generally add more STUFF to each movie. !!! In fact.. hell, I can steal Mafia Vs Ninja footage, say.. for Belly . . . heavily process and distort it . . . Or use some of the backgrounds at least . . . and then key-in masked types. Yeah, this'll give bits of it more of a film quality.

The horrendous waiting and the slight price of super-8 will be gone soon. I'm sure I'll use it once in a while in the future, but for these cheap features with no real crew . . . fuck it. I can get better quality DV-processed-stockfootage-cinelook-etc.

You know, watching a bunch of good low budget films sure did the trick. I've got to remember to do that whenever things on a film shoot get nightmarish. BATHE IN CHEAP MOVIES. It helps point the way, get your skull in proper alignment, leaks motivation, and gives you raw material to modify and rip off.

Test the bluescreen soon and do that LONG TAKE, cutup collage sprinkled in, fake shakespeare play. 5-10 minute entire scenes shot with one camera. Then, cut in random stuff and superimpositions. Definetly a 80 minute feature. 8 segments.

I should probably get a film/video job. September is when I need the studio. Definetly. Today is going to be a great vaguely cold day to shoot . . . Good for masked morons. I think I'll also shoot an outdoor fight sequence with another wrestler.

Film the ninja on the toilet talking to caifano. Use the CB footage If it comes out for the head ninja ordering his goons for the beginning ninja rampage sequence. This would work. So we need plenty of footage of ninja running, slashing, sword unsheathing, and attacking a few people.

Ok, next week try to re-do the bar sequence and get Murray O' Groy's last bits done.

Devil Girls needs insane narration.

I should probably just go get bluescreen paper RIGHT NOW, and then during the week do some intoxico scenes indoors using just the SVHS camera plugged directly into the computer. Key it, then cinelook it, and add it in.

Looks like the plan is to do DV features until I can somehow can afford doing them in 16mm (and have someone else actually operate the camera). Until then, I think this is obviously the way to go. Gotta thank that Mark Pirro guy.

LETTERBOX the el intoxco intro sequence too.

8/3/98 6:09 AM

No shooting yesterday, even though the weather was perfect. Spent the evening editing and wathing that plan nine tape.

Thing is, I don't have a god damn camera. I think what I should do is SEND OUT THE FUCKING ORDER for the video package today, and also head down to brick and buy one of those 80-100 overpriced but WORKING PERFECTLY cameras. This time I'll make sure to get one that does single frame. Also, I can pick up another 2 or 3 rolls of film. Or actually, maybe not. I'll just finish off what I have and switch over to DV when the camera arrives probably something like Friday . . . so next weekend and for the next four weekends this month . . . I definetly get some taping done, as well as during the week. So I'm hoping I can get the film developed before the end of the month, and the video is of course nice and instant...

Also, the fucking projector bulb died. ARGH.

Cinelook isn't perfect but used properly it does add a bit of filmishness to it. The damage is too distracting, turn it on "light". So far I'm happiest with 35mm B&W, using SVHS quality footage it makes a good rough approximation of tri-x Super-8 or 16mm. Not a bad accomplishment at all. So I can shoot some pretty good-looking B&W films. The color I haven't been too enthralled with . . . but hopefully DV footage will help it out a bit so I can maybe get the look of 16mm color . . . which will be just fine for Belly Full of Anger.

Also just noticed I had coincidentally the right-color clay to use for Intoxico. Lots of white, and enough yellow, purple, etc. I can use some of it for the intro sequence. Hmmm, and a bit of grain and frame blending added to the animations would work out pretty well...

Today I'll definetly get a few things done.

"And here's where our screenplay starts to unfold . . . right now..."

Faster

demented A 3 Stooges brutal short. To accompany Belly or Intoxico.

Slight letterboxing helps.

Intoxico is all go. MUST FUCKING FILM FOR SEVERAL DAYS STRAIGHT. Intoxico must be finished at the end of the month.

8/5/98 11:10 PM

Editing first chunk of Rape Lube-Premiere is quite adequate for tossing years of footage together into a propaganda barrage. In time, it'll be nostalgia...

Intoxico is going to probably be a very silly film. I think I'm going to basically reshoot all of it . . . With a Gary Groy character instead of Murray O Groy....

8/7/98 11:33 AM

Well, today is the day to snap out of my lethargy and maybe do some super-8 filming. Yeah, might as well shoot some Ektachrome which I can develop Sunday. Lesse . . . 4 rolls of Ektachrome, 8 rolls of black and white.

8/9/98 9:05 PM

Shooting will definetly commence Wed and thurs, as the load has days off of work. So I those will definetly be two FULL fucking grueling outdoor shoots to break in the camera. Friday is "off", mostly prep work. Sat and Sun some more, if the two Smiths aren't around I'll just do scenes with Groy and Nick etc.

To-Do-or-Desecrate:
Finalize Intoxico costume
NINJA costumes, elaborate and expand
Groy costume
Murray O' Groy's office
Buy pesticide sprayer, corn syrup, food coloring
Ok, I suppose a breakdown is in order. And a script revision. And about a million other things.

This is the most ambitious "project" so far, and I really need to get all the details worked out. None of that "Oh, what do we do now" on the set. Partial storyboards maybe?

God, cinelook takes a long time. As soon as I have footage "in the can", a regular schedule of rendering when I sleep ALL THE TIME must be implemented so I can cut down on waiting around . . . Of course, first I need to see what preset or setting would be the best for the whole damn thing . . . One of the 35mms I imagine. This really could do an incredible job with B&W, but that would make Intoxico that much more difficult to sell. I can save the B&W fetish for Orgy of the Devil Girls. But what really needs to happen is a permanent setup and "staff" for this ministudio. I really need to find more dedicated people to help out . . . These lazy bastards are getting to be a pain to work with . . . Hopefully Intoxico will be received a bit better, reviews or screening will definetly help boost moral.

I think I might have to edit mostly in order . . . adding on 5-10 minute chunks to the DV master as I go along. And since the ending isn't really finalized anyway...

Starting over is pretty irritating, but I think I'm finally over it and ready to make a decent little slice of schlock.

Framing and especially lighting have to be dead-on accurate for cinelook to work it's dubious
magick.

But the most important thing is to do it QUICKLY. This project certainly isn't worth slaving over for years. One month of shooting. One to two months of EDITING. FULL FUCKING

TIME. Crank it out in time for next year's festivals, and while attempting to "market" it . . . GET ON WITH A BELLY FULL OF ANGER!!!!!!

There's simply no excuse for dragging it out . . . it's video, I don't need money . . . I don't need to wait for processing, I have hours of tape, etc.

I just have to make a movie, otherwise I'm going to crack up and kill someone. Trance channeled obsessional filmmaking, with a total disregard for logic and continuity. I just want it to be fast-paced, colorful, gory, silly, melodramatic, overblown, and incredibly overambitious.

Writing scripts or writing filth, it's all the same and it's all the rage. Whether you prance down the main street proudly clutching syd field's latest rapid-eye pontifications on Chinatown . . . or whether you sit slurping cheap lo mein in a demented original spanish/chinese resturaunt hybrid.

8/11/98 12:41 AM

Well, the camera gear arrived unexpectedly today.

Chris/Ian/I watched Astro Zombies, Orgy of the Dead, and assorted Russ Meyer whilst frying and testing out the spiffy camera. I like it-it's tiny, but with the right light the quality is pretty good.

Tommorow is preperation, and then wed. is our initiation day of Intoxico taping.

This camera is also perfect to continue my diaryesque RL/Nature's On/Junky's Birfday sort of Super-8 work, only much cheaper. Too bad I don't have a frame by frame mode . . . Actually, I can easily do this by using premiere in stop motion mode when digitizing. Versatile, useful stuff. I have no idea why I sticked with murky, expensive super-8. The grain and scratches are nice, but definetly not worth hundreds of dollars of lost footage. FUCK! But fucked rebirth, new equipment always provides a burst of creativity. This camera is going to be a constant companion for the next few years. I'm going to end up with hundreds of hours of excrutiatingly dull footage along with "the good stuff"

I love this camera. When I first plugged it in downstairs, I wasn't stricken just yet, I was actually lamenting the purchase . . . But once the feature set was rubberbanded and compounded, the value is apparent. This takes over RL filming. RL will be hours long, actually.

A perfect way to continue the diary work.

I can see why George Kuchar got into video cameras for trash journals-

NOTE: Ninja HQ interior: do this with the FULL size of the garage, with some sort of cheap covering. It needs all sorts of junk around, the old computer, monitors, CB, blenders, etc. Lots of detail. A ninja corpse lies on a wooden table, tubes connect it to automotive equipment and assorted gimmicks.

Spew:

Horribly mismatched day and night shots

Boring science talk-gack, the ninja are zombies of course.

When they remove their hoods, blue makeup, circles under the eyes, theatrical–looking and silly . . . latex clumps randomly applied . . . PERFECT, Intoxico can remove the hood, a trumpet blasts and it zooms in.

Chairman goes off into a long villanous tirade concerning nothing in particular ending with the overzealous evil man knocking over a bunch of equipment or possibly punching out the assistant ninja.

The long hallucination sequence will be perfect . . . Starting with subtle distortion and flo-motion, then color offsetting in-sanely, kaleidescopic intoxico heads screaming, claymation horrors bluescreened in.... Menacing guys in masks running around (use up the rest of the mask reserve for this-they all make cameos . . . Looped Murray O' Groy admonitions superimposed on top of Intoxico gasping and pawing at his face. Eventually he imagines he's running through a field on his hands and knees...the sky changes colors and the glow effect is used plenty of times-In fact this would be a good way to pad out 8-10 minutes with an incred-ibly long nonsensically surreal intermission about 40 minutes into the movie . . . Definetly before the "final onslaught" of the HQ.

"Prepare for total astro-mobilization!"

-John Carradine, "Astro-Zombies"

Astro zombies has obviously given me the above ranting. Stitching movies together and collaging them-pretty much my current style in other areas, and it works sort of well in film-This script at least didn't take years to write.

Let me repeat, and always REMEMBER TO DO THIS LATER ON (when and if stuck or lifeless) WATCHING LOW BUDGET EXPLOITATION MOVIES strengthens der morale and really helps you to "focus" . . . I imagine that the huge influx of HGL/Santo/Ninja/JapaneseTrash/Wood I'll be swallowing during most of this week will really invigorate and defenestrate. The last third of the movie and a bunch of earlier (tacked on in the appropriate places and PADDED OUT) scenes will be written every night due to this. In fact, let me repeat what I supposedly promised to do a few days ago and only feebly complied: one scene or at least a few ideas for potential scenes every night before tired sleep...

8/11/98 1:00 PM

"Who needs good film in this business, anyway?"

-Ed Wood, "The Sinister Urge"

Have Murray O' Groy consult Ashish Sheth for his computer-induced "research" on the ninja problem.....

Santo in a business suit interacting with the public or in a public place.

8/12/98 11:57 PM

Did absolutely nothing today. Shameful, really.

I'm right at the start of Night of the Ghouls . . . ah, pristine and beautiful new Ed Wood experience . . . With plenty of Criswell, which I of course must sample...

GAH! Just found that on the web. FINALLY! I can't wait to take a look at Devil Girls . . . I think I'll freely adapt it and mutate, mixing Wood with Woodesque, stock footage with stock writing, in a patchwork on-the-cheap sort of way that Ed would have loved. In fact, this might have to be a 16mm B&W job to really do it justice. We'll see. Maybe DV/cinelook will suffice.

[ED. NOTE: So very sad.]

You paint your wallpapers green-

Twisted carcass uprooting from the sour felt of an elvis eimpersonator with a taste for the imperious nature of his only fixture: that of scientology's science guy's oblivion tracking shot-East . . . Cut west and lunge across the plain-shadows lie in waiting for their true directorial debut and 3 picture deal with supposed independents . . . Hollywood granting money occasionally, but this must take place outside of their rigid system. If I have to suffer in Hoboken, so be it. My temperment is better suited to urban starvation anyway, at least until I get mellow in my mid 30s and decide to move out to some farm in the middle of nowhere for isolation between work cycles. But I'm getting ahead of myself here. And when you get ahead of yourself it's usually best to stop for a few seconds and calm down, calm yourself and calm your remains before the circus continues-the barker twirls around and strikes-stop striking you twisted fucker-ouch, as I fall back alongside the path..... Carnival barkers are a dime a dozen and four circles to a pound, anyway. We all know they lack critical skills in general to twist their own graves—Spinning semicircles, obsessions with circles in general and keeping vision straight. Vision is always straight-if sometimes darting off to look to the side—side side side-look to the side and you'll see why-sideways circles lighting up-sideways splendor marks marker construction . . . John Deere, If you could see him now-John Deere, a fallen man and icon for his judgement. John Deere, ponderous manufacturer of the American Dream-the dream you see under heavy lidded eyes at the side of the road at some 1am drive back home along the back roads, nerves on alert and dreading the bit of road past the police station-why? There's nothing contraband, or if there is . . . Chances are slim of an encounter. But you're on guard anyway, on guard and on patrol, trying not to shuffle gloomily past the ticket takers. Get your tickets here, get your tickets here.

Dodging and character avoidance, a look at preservation-that's what characterizes the preceeding pages-overblown tales of modern

living sauced with noise-the noise that really won't result in anything, but dear bob is it entertaining to listen to once in a while and to play . . . I haven't played for the past few months, suddenly just stopped-concentrating on film and of course once my net presence was back I . . . I just avoided turning on the ever present 4-track that now lies full of feedback-dormant and unplugged-too lazy to reconnect it, I suppose. As if it would take that much effort. Then there are the thousand tapes-dozens and dozens of sessions, several "bands" . . . cds and cds full of material that I'll never get to organizing . . . I keep creating without pausing to survey what I passed, what roads I already travelled on . . . Once the dirt covers the trail I'm not there anymore-I'm on the next bit, or wasting time around the next bit . . . That laying around time-I enjoy being lazy just a little too much. Days will pass, end to end passive mouse clicking punctuated by infrequent attempts at keeping a schedule. At least I finally gained enough of a journal habit to jot things down MOST of the time . . . Writing at night . . . Typing the meager hopes that passed—And when the door closes all that will be left, well I say that as if it's minimal . . . thousands of hours, pages of text and bad art, hours of film and video-For 22 I haven't done too bad for myself so far. It's getting the publicity. Exploitation-showmanship-spin a dream and watch the people try to get a hold of it . . . But they're left scratching their eyes and holding on to their own dreams . . . Tattered remains of what they thought they were grabbing.

Frayed edges, the usual antsyness . . . what exactly am I waiting for that will be better than my present situation? Calm the hell down.

Concentration and focus: badly fucking needed.

9/7/98 11:31 PM

Watching Tetsuo.

Wasted a lot of time on the internet-sucking entity. Starting with Intoxico rudeness again, Thursday afternoon . . . I figure tonight I'll make a pass at the script and get it in order for at least some quick scenes this week. Next week whatshisname gets that house so I bet a lot of filming will be done there . . . We can take a bedroom and really badly set decorate the hell out of it. Plus filming on the beach near there...

As far as the next inhibitors disc goes, I have enough to do probably half of the album using the two sessions we noisedouted, Yodobo II, and those tapes of unfinished solo synth doodlings. Sprinkle in several hundred samples and there you go.

Well, I probably should stop this nonsense and start editing now.

Here we go, starting with the basic noise tracks from 9/4/98 "Dracula vs Frankenstein" Soundtrack.

"Reality itself is the grandest illusion of all"

EPILOGUE.

And with that completely unrelated note, we end this fine volume of decadence, wasted time, and boring hooded "wrestling".

We hope we have succeeded in crushing your childhood film-making dreams and confidence in the future.

Please contact us if you are in need of further assistance.

Regards,

Coleman T. Craig

bmmedia consumption liason

bowleggedmanmedia.com